DL 119

Writing Through the Year

Building Confident Writers One Month at a Time

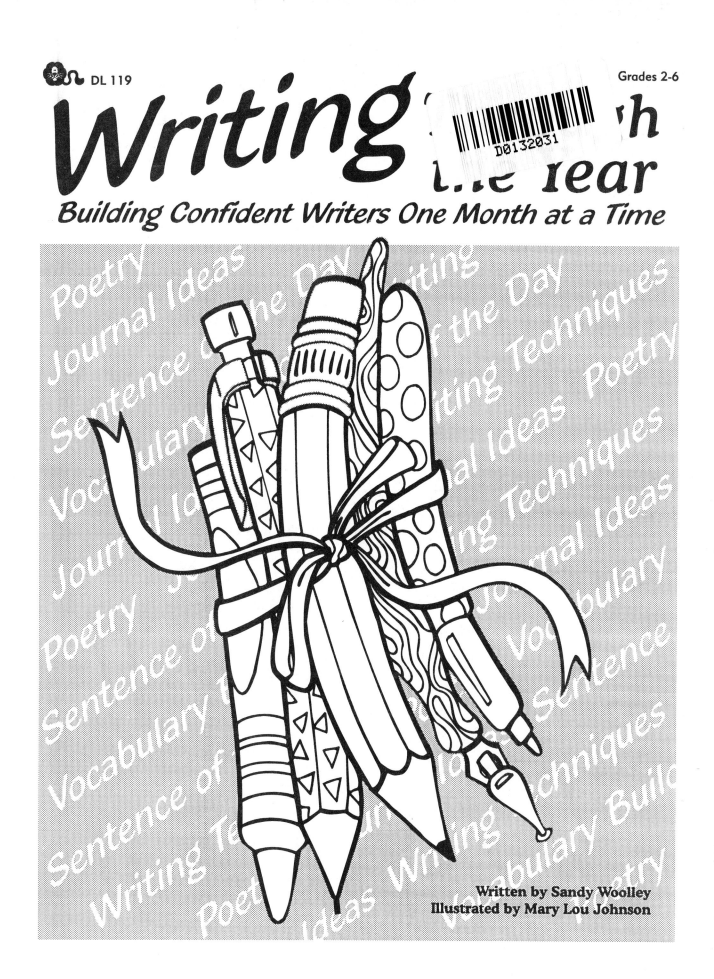

Written by Sandy Woolley
Illustrated by Mary Lou Johnson

Edited by Dianne Draze and Sonsie Conroy

ISBN 1-883055-27-X

Dandy Lion Publications
P.O. Box 190
San Luis Obispo, CA 93406

Contents

About This Book

Good writing is a combination of skills that are learned and practiced throughout one's life. While grammar is important, good writing is not just knowing when to use a comma, capital letter, or quotation marks. It is being able to organize your thoughts so they make sense to someone else, being able to to call forth a rich and varied vocabulary, being able to describe things so that others can visualize just what you experienced, being able to string words together so that they sing, and being able to tell a story in a way that others will find intensely interesting. Like many other talents, good writing is developed with instruction, critique, and practice. Those people who write, become better writers. Those people who do not write, have little chance of developing their writing talents.

Writing skills are developed by writing on a daily basis, and when we can give our students many different writing experiences, we are building these writing skills. This book presents several different aspects of a complete writing program. For each month of the school year, you are given ideas for sentences of the day, journal writing, poetry, vocabulary development, and different writing skills. The rationale is to give students a wide variety of writing experiences; experiences that allow them to work on the rules of grammar, to develop the ability to present ideas with clarity and organization, to think creatively, and to try out the richness of the written word. These exercises are designed to improve students' writing skills in a developmental manner, with each month building on the previous month's work and introducing new writing forms. By working through the year this way and giving students regular opportunities to write, by the end of the year you should have a classroom of competent writers who are eager to write and know they are skillful.

Sentence of the Day

Using a daily sentence is a good way to polish grammar skills and start the day in an orderly fashion. As school begins, have a sentence or sentences on the board or overhead projector ready for the students as they enter the classroom. This sentence will have incorrect punctuation and capitalization. It may have incorrect spelling, incorrect homonyms, and incorrect grammar, as well. The students' job is to sit down and copy this sentence or sentences onto their papers, correcting all mistakes as they work.

Student Involvement

On your desk you should have a name can. This is a can that has each child's name on a popsicle stick or tongue depressor. It is a fair way of making certain that each child has a turn and that all students are paying attention, because they don't know when their name will be called. When you see that most students have completed the corrections, pull names out of the can one at a time. Have each student come up and make a correction on the board or overhead. This is best done with another color of chalk. The student's job is to also tell why this correction is being made. He or she may say something like, "It is the beginning of a sentence," "Commas are used in a series," or "We always capitalize nationalities."

Choosing Sentences

Included in each month's ideas are suggested sentences for sentences of the day. The sentences are written correctly. You should use the basic information and sentence to structure sentences with mistakes or omissions that reflect the ability level of your students. Many of these sentences relate historical events that are interesting and educational. Change these basic sentences to fit any punctuation and capitalization skills you are studying, making them easier if necessary. You may wish to also include your own sentences about events in your school or community.

Adjusting the Difficulty of the Sentences

There are three ways to deal with any sentences that are too difficult for your students and/or that contain corrections they haven't learned yet. You could do one of the following:

1. Change the sentence to make it appropriate.

2. Put in any appropriate corrections and point them out to students.

3. Explain that there is a correction to be made that is very difficult and that you don't expect anyone to know it because it is one they would normally learn in a higher grade. Then ask if anyone would like to try to make the correction. Someone usually gets the correction and is incredibly proud. If not, make the correction yourself and briefly explain it.

With second graders you may wish to make up your own sentences for the first half of the year. These would be sentences that pertain to the subject matter you are studying in science, social studies, and math. It's always fun for the students to have their names included. When you feel they are ready, begin to include the ideas in some of the primary sentence-of-the-day sentences.

Record Keeping

The students should keep their sentence-of-the-day paper in their desks Monday through Thursday, adding the sentences each day. On Thursday, after they complete their sentence and corrections have been discussed, have them put their papers in their binders to study that evening. On Friday give them a test paper that has all the sentences for the week without corrections. This is a good way to see in what areas students show competence and in what areas they need more work the following week. It is an excellent way to make certain that everyone understands the grammar rules. It gives you immediate feedback, and a surprise benefit is that everyone knows exactly what to do as they enter the room, adding to a quiet, focused beginning of the day.

For each month you will find examples of historical events that happened on each day. These are fun to use because the students enjoy reading about them. These should be modified to fit the grade level and skill areas the class may be working on. Other sentences that are effective are sentences pertaining to the social studies or science units you're studying. The students enjoy seeing their names on their birthdays. If you can find an author who was also born on their day, it is especially fun to have a sentence that says:

(too, two, to) important authors were born on march 27 one of them was dick king smith author of babe the other one was tommy jones fifth grader from room 15 and superior science whiz

Grade Level Expectations

Every school district and state will differ on what it expects students at a particular grade level to know, but here are some standards that may help you if you do not have a district continuum.

✶ Second Grade

By the end of **second grade** students should be expected to use the following correctly.

They should be able to capitalize:

- the names of people and pets
- the word "I"
- the names of towns, cities, states, and countries
- the names of days, months, holidays, and other special days
- the names of streets and roads
- the first word in every sentence
- important words in titles
- the first word in the greeting and closing of a letter.

They should be able to use a comma:

- between the day of the month and the year
- between a city and state or city and country
- after the greeting and closing of a letter

They should be able to use a period at the end of a statement.

They should be able to use a question mark at the end of a question.

They should be able to use an exclamation point at the end of an exclamation.

✶ Third Grade

By the end of **third grade** students should be expected to use all of the above correctly as well as the following.

They should be able to capitalize:

- initials
- the names of continents
- a person's title and the abbreviation of a title
- the names of special buildings
- the first word of a quotation
- the first word in every line of most poems
- the first word, the last word, and every other important word in a title

They should be able to use a comma in a series.

They should be able to use a period in the abbreviations of titles and other common abbreviations.

They should be able to use an apostrophe:

- for contractions
- for singular possessives

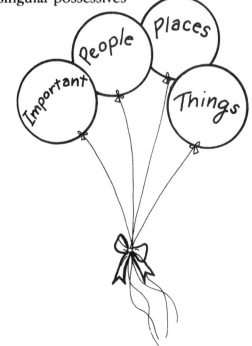

7

✷ Fourth Grade

By the end of **fourth grade** students should be expected to use all of the above correctly as well as the following.

They should be able to capitalize the first word, and every other important word in a title of a book or a movie.

They should be able to use commas:

- to set off direct quotations from the rest of the sentence
- after "yes" or "no" at the beginning of a sentence.
- after the name of the person spoken to.
- after the first complete thought in a sentence with two thoughts (before the conjunctions like "and," "but," or "because")

They should be able to use a period after each numeral or letter that shows a division for an outline.

They should be able to use quotation marks for titles of poems, stories, reports, and other short works.

They should be able to underline the titles of books, magazines, movie titles, and other long works.

✷ Fifth Grade

By the end of **fifth grade** students should be expected to use all of the above correctly as well as the following.

They should be able to capitalize:

- titles of magazines, documents, etc.
- the names of religions
- the names of businesses, clubs, and organizations

They should be able to use quotation marks in dialogue.

They should be able to use an apostrophe to show the possessive of a plural noun.

✷ Sixth Grade

By the end of **sixth grade** students should be expected to use all of the above correctly as well as the following.

They should be able to use commas to set off an appositive (interrupter) in a sentence.

They should be able to use a hyphen in compound numbers from twenty-one through ninety-nine.

They should be able to use a colon:

- after the greeting in a business letter.
- between the numerals that tell the hours and minutes.

They should be able to use a semicolon to combine two related sentence when the semicolon takes the place of both the comma and the conjunction.

Journal Writing

Why Include Journal Writing?

Journal writing is the practice that students need at least twice a week to help them learn to clarify their thoughts and organize them into a short but interesting statements. With journals everyone is writing on the same subject, yet the entries differ greatly. The topics usually allow students to interject themselves into their writing by discussing their favorite things or situations they have experienced. This writing is not as developed as fictional stories, but it should still be organized and descriptive. By writing on a regular basis, students develop fluency and can experiment with new vocabulary or different arrangements of words and ideas.

Sharing Writing

You may choose to have students share their journal writing. By listening to interesting entries of other students, students also learn to expand their writing and to be descriptive. If Toby has written, *"My favorite breakfast is cereal and juice,"* and hears Maria read, *"I always enjoy hot oatmeal sprinkled with brown sugar. When the creamy milk is poured on top, there is a delightful taste of hot and cold melted together. With my oatmeal I love fresh squeezed orange juice."* Toby may look at his writing and see how to write better next time. It is this constant improvement that helps our students become better writers.

A Tried and True System

I have tried many different ideas for journal writing. This is the idea that works best for me and seems to produce the most positive results for my students.

The journals are a folded piece of construction paper with the name of the month and various appropriate designs printed on the cover. On each page of this book that has journal ideas is artwork that would be appropriate to use on the cover of a journal. Purchase of this book gives you the right to duplicate this artwork for journals to use in your classroom.

Inside the folder I staple about eight sheets of lined paper. We write in the journals on a given topic twice a week, usually right after "Sentence of the Day." I usually give the students about ten minutes to complete their entries, depending on the subject. When they write, they start with the date in the upper right corner, as one might start a letter. They then use what I have written on the board as their first sentence (unless they would like to reword it). As they write, I usually wander around the room, making certain that ideas are going on the paper and clarifying the assignment for those who are uncertain about it. During the first month the dreaded "Is this long enough?" question comes up. My answer is, "Did you say everything you wanted in a complete and interesting way?" and "Is it ___th grade quality?" When most of the students are finished I ask for volunteers to read their entries aloud. Usually there are many people who want to share their work. I try to make positive comments orally about great descriptive writing and particular words that were strong.

Reviewing the Journals

At the end of the month these journals are collected and new ones are passed out. I then read each entry and make written comments back to the child. I don't give a grade on the journal itself, but I give two grades in my grade book: a grade for punctuation and capitalization and a grade for style, ideas, clarity, and creativity. I often will write myself a note in the grade book so I can share a positive comment about the child's writing with a parent. By reading the journals you learn a great deal about your students. After you have read all the entries, you have a better understanding of things that are not always mentioned in class.

Journal Writing Ideas

This book includes ideas for journal writing for most of the months. The one for November also combines December due to the number of holidays in the two months. Students follow the same procedure from September to February, but by March the students begin to get bored with the assignment, so the journal assignment changes for the months of March and April. See these months for further details. May and June are also combined. There are several journal topics given for each month. It will, of course, depend on the grade level you're teaching as to which are appropriate.

* * * * * * * * * * * * * * * * * * * *

Vocabulary

Vocabulary development is an important writing skill, because part of writing is having an arsenal of words at your fingertips that you use to express your ideas. One easy way to build vocabulary is to learn the building blocks that make up words. When we teach root words, prefixes, or suffixes, we are teaching the meaning of several words. When a student understands that *pre* means "before," words like "precaution," "predict," and "prevent" make much more sense. If they see *hydro* or *hydra* and know that it means "water," then "hydraulic," "hydroplane," "dehydrate," and "hydrant" are logical.

Teaching the Building Blocks

How do we teach these word building blocks? One way is to feature one root, prefix, or suffix on a bulletin board each week or month and have students add words as they find them during their free time. At the end of each day or week, have the class see if each word on the board is truly made up of the root, prefix, or suffix and see if anyone can figure out the meaning.

Another method is to give the root and some related words each week as a vocabulary lesson. Just as a spelling list is introduced on Monday, vocabulary words are studied during the week, and a test is given on Friday, you could do the same with these vocabulary words. You can also have students study and use vocabulary words in context throughout the week and test them on their meaning at the end of the week.

For students in lower grades, you will want to select the easier words from the list. When presenting the root, suffix, or prefix, talk about what it means and then ask them what words they already know that contain this word builder. This will give you an idea of which words you can present that will be new and challenging. Present only a few words each week.

* * * * * * * * * * * * * * * * * * * *

Poetry

Poems to Memorize

Why memorize poems? If you include this aspect of poetry study in your curriculum, you will find that years later students still remember the wonderful poems that they memorized in your class and can still recite them. That alone isn't a good enough reason, however, to memorize poems. There are other reasons. One is that practice speaking in front of others is a skill students will use over and over again in life. Those individuals who don't present to groups before they are in middle school or high school are not as comfortable as those who speak before the class monthly. Memorized poetry, with its rhyme and rhythm, is easier to master and present than an essay speech (whether it is one that the student has written or one from a famous person in history). Too, what a terrific opportunity this is to become familiar with poets and their diverse works. Once students have memorized poems by several poets, they start to get a feel for many different forms of poetry and this helps them write their own poems.

Writing Poetry

The poetry section also includes ideas for writing poems each month. In some months there are several ideas, so you can pick which ideas are most appropriate. Several traditional poetry forms, like cinquain and haiku, are presented; but there are also several ideas for changing the words in existing poems. This is an effective way to get students started writing poems. The poems usually do not have to rhyme. Students need only supply descriptive words and phrases to match the format or rhythm of the sample poem. You will be surprised at the quality of writing you get with these poems.

Sentence of the Day

Monday _____
_____
_____
_____

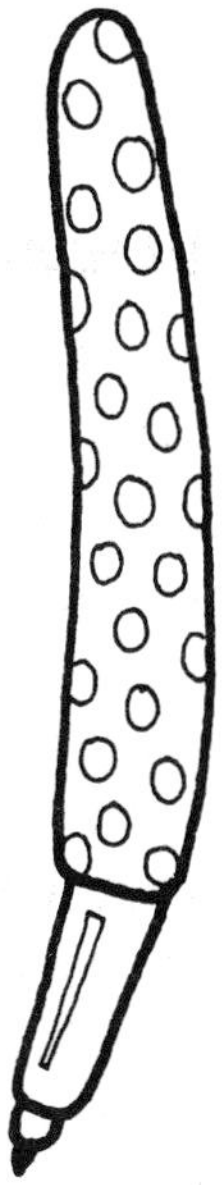

Tuesday _____
_____
_____
_____

WEDNESDAY _____
_____
_____
_____

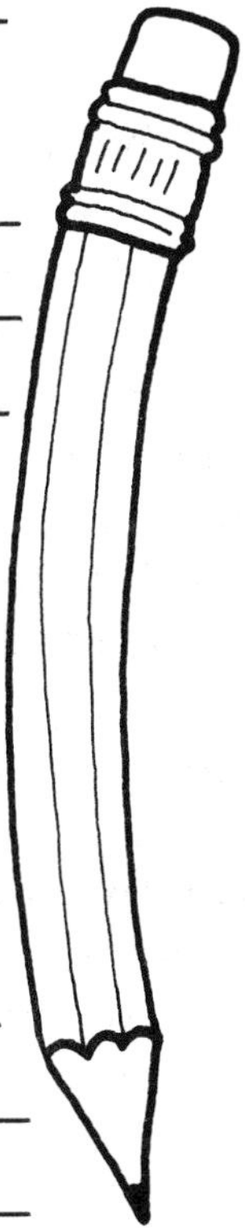

Thursday _____
_____
_____
_____

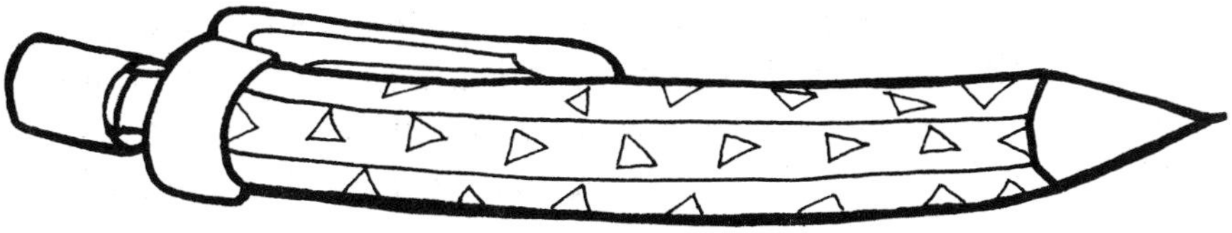

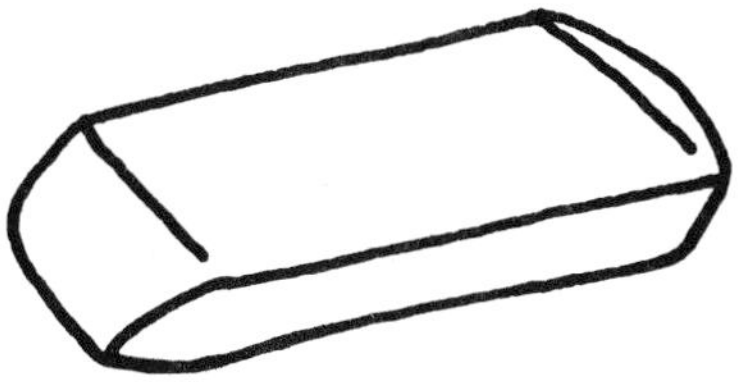

Primary

- September is the ninth month of the year. It was the seventh month in the old Roman calendar, and its name comes from the Latin word *septem*, meaning "seven." Julius Caesar changed the calendar to make the year begin on January 1 instead of March 1.
- September has thirty days. The September flower is the aster, and the birthstone is the sapphire.
- *Rosh Hashanah* and *Yom Kippur* are two important Jewish holidays. They fall in the months of September or October.
- The first Monday in September is Labor Day. It is a day to honor American workers.

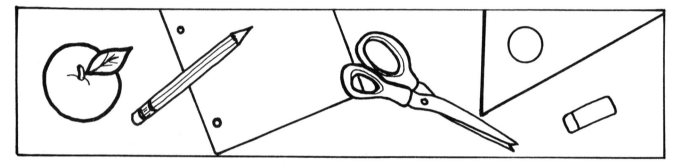

1. Edgar Rice Burroughs was born on September 1, 1875. He wrote <u>Tarzan.</u>

2. The first week in September is National Dog Week.

4. In 1888 George Eastman patented the first roll film camera. It took 100 pictures.

7. This is the birthday of Grandma Moses. She was a famous American artist.

7. On September 7, 1896, in Cranston, Rhode Island, the first automobile race on a track was held.

8. The United Nations observes this day as International Literacy Day in honor of worldwide reading.

8. The Pledge of Allegiance was first read on September 8, 1892.

9. California became a state on this day in 1850.

10. After working on it for five years, Elias Howe patented the sewing machine on this day in 1846.

12. Jesse Owens was a famous Olympic gold medal winner who won his medals in 1936.

13. This is the birthday of Milton Hershey. He is famous for Hershey's chocolates.

14. In 1814 Francis Scott Key wrote "The Star Spangled Banner." It is our national anthem.

15. Two famous authors have their birthdays today. They are Tomie De Paola and Robert McCloskey.

16. This is Mexico's Independence Day.

16. In 1620 Pilgrims sailed on the <u>Mayflower</u> from England. It took them three months to sail across the Atlantic Ocean.

16. On this day in 1916 Roald Dahl was born. He wrote <u>Charlie and the Chocolate Factory.</u>

17. Our Constitution was signed on this day in 1787.

19. The Montgolfier brothers sent a duck, a sheep, and a rooster up in a balloon in 1796.

20. Sister Elizabeth Kenny developed a method of treating polio. She was born on this day in 1886.

21. This is usually the first day of autumn. On this day there are twelve hours of night and twelve hours of day.

23. The planet Neptune was discovered on this day in 1846. It takes about 165 years to revolve around the sun.

25. Balboa discovered the Pacific Ocean on this day in 1513.

26. Johnny Chapman was born on this day in 1774. He is known to us as Johnny Appleseed.

29. This is the birthday of Stan Berenstain, author of the Berenstain Bears books.

30. The last Friday in September is called Native American Day in honor of Native Americans.

Upper Grades

- September is the ninth month of the year. It was the seventh month in the old Roman calendar, and its name comes from the Latin word *septem*, meaning "seven." Julius Caesar changed the calendar to make the year begin on January 1 instead of March 1.

- September has thirty days. The September flower is the aster, and the September birthstone is the sapphire.

- *Rosh Hashanah* and *Yom Kippur*, two important Jewish holidays, fall in the months of September or October.

- The first Monday in September is Labor Day. It was first observed in New York City on September 5, 1882. It became a national holiday in 1894 when President Grover Cleveland signed a bill making it a legal holiday. It is a day to honor American workers.

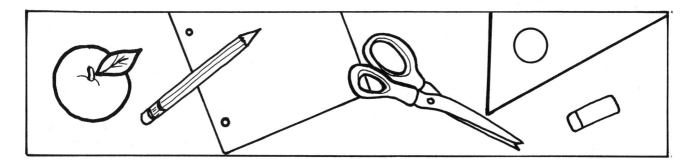

1. On this day in 1939 German troops tore down barriers along the Polish border and crossed into Poland, invading it and starting World War II.

2. The United States Department of the Treasury was established in 1789. This department prepares all paper money, coins, and federal securities.

2. On this day in 1666 the Great Fire of London broke out in a baker's house, destroying 13,000 houses. It lasted four days.

2. Over 1,500,000 British children were evacuated from their homes near cities to stay with families in the country. This was done in September, 1939, in fear that German planes might bomb cities in England if a war started.

3. On this day in 1783 Great Britain signed the Treaty of Paris, ending the Revolutionary War in America.

4. On September 4, 1888, George Eastman of Rochester, New York patented the first roll film camera. This camera used a roll of 100 exposures.

5. The First Continental Congress assembled in Philadelphia in 1774. It was attended by fifty-six delegates representing twelve colonies. The first Congress was more interested in fair treatment from Great Britain than in independence.

6. Jane Addams was born on this day in 1860. She received the Nobel Peace Prize in 1931. She was an American social worker and humanitarian.

7. Grandma Moses was born on September 7, 1860. She started painting when she was seventy-eight. Even though she never had an art lesson, she is respected as a fine American painter.

7. On this day in 1896 A. H. Whiting won the first automobile race on a track. The race was held in Cranston, Rhode Island. The winning speed was twenty-four miles per hour.

8. September 8 is observed by the United Nations as International Literacy Day. This is to honor reading worldwide.

9. General Lafayette of France was born on this day in 1757. Lafayette volunteered to serve the United States during the Revolutionary War. He spent much personal time and his fortune to aid the United States.

9. California became the thirty-first state on this date in 1850.

10. On this day in 1846 Elias Howe patented the sewing machine. Previously he had worked as a machinist and cotton mill worker in Massachusetts. His invention took five years to perfect.

12. Henry Hudson entered the river named for him on this day in 1609.

12. This is the birthday of Jesse Owens, the American athlete who set three world records and tied another at the 1936 Olympic Games in Berlin. He was a record holder in jumping, sprinting, and hurdling. He was born in 1913 and died in 1980.

13. Author Roald Dahl was born on this day in 1916. He is the author of <u>Charlie and the Chocolate Factory</u>, <u>James and the Giant Peach</u>, and many other adult and children's books and stories.

13. Margaret Chase Smith became the first woman elected to the United States Senate without having served a prior appointed term. Before being elected to the Senate in 1948, she had served as a U.S. representative.

14. On this day in 1814 Francis Scott Key wrote our national anthem, "The Star Spangled Banner." He did this after witnessing the British bombardment of Fort McHenry.

14. In 1752 King George of England proclaimed that today would be September 14, 1752. The interesting thing about this was that the day before had been September 2, 1752. Why did he do this? He did it because the calendar was off and needed to be corrected.

15. September 15, 1857 is the birth date of William Howard Taft, the twenty-seventh president of the United States. He started the custom of the president throwing out the first ball to start the baseball season each year.

15. Agatha Christie, famous mystery writer, was born in 1890. She wrote about eighty detective novels and several plays. Like most authors, she had many rejections before any publisher bought her work.

16. On this day in 1620 English emigrants set sail from Plymouth, England on the <u>Mayflower</u> to sail to what is now America.

16. September 16, 1810, is Mexico's Independence Day. Before independence, Mexico had been ruled by Spain for 300 years.

17. Constitution Week begins on September 17 with Constitution Day. This document was signed on September 17, 1787. It replaced the Articles of Confederation.

18. Samuel Johnson, English author of the dictionary, was born on this day in 1709.

18. French scientist Jean Bernard Leon Foucault was born on this day in 1819. He is famous for inventing the gyroscope.

19. On this day in 1796, George Washington's farewell address was published.

19. In 1783 the Montgolfier brothers sent up the first balloon with live creatures on board. There was a sheep, a rooster, and a duck.

20. On this day in 1519, Ferdinand Magellan, a Portuguese explorer, set forth on his three-year voyage around the world. Although five ships  started, only one returned. Magellan, however, was not among those who went home. He had been killed in the Philippines.

20. Sister Elizabeth Kenny, an Australian nurse, developed a method of treating polio. She was born on this day in 1886.

22. On this day in 1776, at twenty-one, Nathan Hale was put to death as a spy by the British. Before he was executed he made a speech, concluding with these words, "I only regret that I have but one life to lose for my country." He is considered an American hero and patriot.

21. This day is usually the beginning of autumn. On this day there are twelve hours of night and twelve of day.

23. Victoria Claflin Woodhull was born on this day in 1838. She was the first woman to run for president of the United States. She fought for women's rights.

23. The planet Neptune was discovered on this day in 1846. This planet takes about 165 years to revolve around the sun.

24. Wilson Rawls, author of <u>Summer of the Monkeys</u> and <u>Where the Red Fern Grows</u>, was born on this day in 1913.

25. One September 25, 1513, Vasco Nuñez de Balboa, a Spanish explorer, became the first European to see the eastern shore of the Pacific Ocean. He claimed the ocean for Spain and renamed it the Pacific, meaning "peaceful."

25. Sandra Day O'Connor was sworn in as the first female justice of the Supreme Court on this date in 1981.

26. This is the birth date of John Chapman, better known as Johnny Appleseed. He is considered the first planter of orchards across America. He was born in 1774 and died in March, 1845 near Fort Wayne, Indiana.

26. On this date in 1580 Francis Drake and fifty sailors of the <u>Golden Hind</u> became the first Englishmen to circumnavigate the earth. Their voyage lasted thirty-three months.

26. This is the birth date of Thomas Stearns Eliot. He was known as T. S. Eliot. He was a famous American poet. One of his books was made into the musical, <u>Cats</u>.

27. Samuel Adams, the great American patriot, was born on this day in 1722. He was a leading spokesman for American Independence. His speeches and his writings stirred discontent among the colonists before the Revolutionary War. He signed the Declaration of Independence.

27. Hiram Rhodes Revels was born on this day in 1822. He was the first black man to become a United States senator. He represented Mississippi.

29. The first football game to be played at night took place on this date in 1892 at Mansfield Fair in Mansfield, Pennsylvania.

Words to Sentences

The Beginning Assignment

Begin the year by making every student in your class feel that this is the grade in which he or she will be a fine writer. Who could resist this assignment:

Write a sentence that includes the words dragon, moat, and castle. You may include any other words you wish and dragon, moat, and castle may be in any order, but it must be only one sentence.

After being given these three words, almost everyone will immediately begin writing and will be anxious to share his or her sentence. For some students this is a breakthrough. They are suddenly writers and sharers of their writing!

Additional Challenges

When students have written their first sentence, continue the challenge and vary the assignment with the following variations:

1. This time "dragon" must be the third word in the sentence. This will lead to adjectives being used because students usually will write sentences that begin like, "The large dragon" or "The scaly dragon. . ." This will give you a chance to praise the use of descriptive writing.

2. Use the same rules as the previous assignment with the addition of the rule: Make your sentence different from anyone else's in the class. Use the words "footprints," "muddy," and "prince."

3. Try the same thing with "castle," "gigantic," and "damp."

4. Use the word "summer" in a sentence. Once again, make it different than anyone else's.

5. Write a six-word sentence using your name as the fourth word.

6. Try making the assignment harder by giving the students three seemingly unrelated words like "bicycle," "horrible," and "diamond."

7. Write a sentence that does not contain the word "cold" but gives us the idea of coldness.

8. Using commas in the correct places, write a sentence telling us what your three favorite ice cream flavors are.

9. Use "stars," "twinkle," and "sunset" in an interesting sentence.

10. Use "September," "new friends," and "school" in a sentence. Try to make it unlike anyone else's.

Adding Variety

Add your own ideas to these suggestions and spread the assignments over a period of two weeks. Don't cover more than a few ideas each day. You want the students to groan when it's time to stop and cheer when it's time to take out the paper and work on a few more.

This type of activity is a wonderful way to check for understanding in the areas of math, social studies, or science. If you are studying explorers, for example, ask the students to write a paragraph with only true facts that includes "Columbus," "Magellan," and "da Gama." While adding elements from other areas of the curriculum remember that, the object of this assignment, of course, is to get students to write complete, interesting, and descriptive sentences and to understand how words might be moved around for variety and interest.

Experts of the Dictionary

September is a great time to teach dictionary skills in your classroom. Although most teachers feel that students should not be expected to look up every word they need to know how to spell, it is important that they can use the dictionary with ease if they need to.

Experts is a fun and positive experience. For some classes, you may wish to let students have a partner. It doesn't take away from the learning experience and it makes it more enjoyable. Answers for the worksheets appear on page 125.

1. A first step is to pass out a dictionary to every child. If they try to find the exact middle of the book by carefully dividing it in half, they will probably land on the letter *l* or *m*. They then are able to find any word starting with these two letters with ease and any word that begins with *k* or *n* since these two come immediately before and after *l* and *m*.

2. Step two is to take the first half and divide it in half. They will probably open to *c* or *d*. At this point the students will begin to see that each time they need a word they don't need to go through every page to find it.

3. Step three is to do the same thing with the second half of the book. If they are looking for the middle of this section, they will probably open to *r* or *s*. Now see how quickly the students can find the letter *m*, then *d*, then *c*, then *s*, etc. Something that could be a boring exercise becomes a fun adventure.

4. Once they have become confident with dictionary skills, and you have discussed the use of the words at the top of the page (guide words), how some words have several meanings listed, and how, when looking for a word, the second, third, and even fourth letters of that word may be important, they are then ready to become an expert. Students become *Experts of the Dictionary* by completing three worksheets correctly. Once they have completed the first sheet they are novices, after the second sheet they are apprentices, and after the third sheet they become experts. When a student has completed the third level, he or she is then ready to do a self-portrait with an expert emblem drawn on his or her shirt. These self portraits can then go on a bulletin board with the other students' drawings.

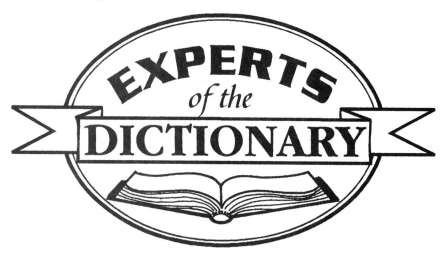

Experts of the Dictionary
Novice

Name _____

Find each word in the dictionary and
write the page number beside the word.
Then decide whether you would wear
this thing or travel in it. Write wear or
travel on the line in the right column.

Word	page	*wear* or TRAVEL
1. sulky	_____	_____
2. gondola	_____	_____
3. surrey	_____	_____
4. hansom	_____	_____
5. doublet	_____	_____
6. howdah	_____	_____
7. ascot	_____	_____
8. kilt	_____	_____
9. epaulet	_____	_____
10. obi	_____	_____
11. fez	_____	_____
12. kayak	_____	_____
13. toboggan	_____	_____
14. umiak	_____	_____
15. jerkin	_____	_____
16. jodhpurs	_____	_____
17. victoria	_____	_____
18. derby	_____	_____

Experts of the Dictionary
Apprentice

Name _____

Find each word in the dictionary and write the page number beside the word. Then write each word in the correct box below.

1. lute	p. ____	8. oboe	p. ____
2. orb	p. ____	9. scull	p. ____
3. frets	p. ____	10. pharynx	p. ____
4. yawl	p. ____	11. sitar	p. ____
5. gaff	p. ____	12. prow	p. ____
6. sternum	p. ____	13. fife	p. ____
7. palate	p. ____	14. viola	p. ____

15. zither	p. ____
16. ulna	p. ____
17. dulcimer	p. ____
18. tacking	p. ____
19. piccolo	p. ____
20. epiglottis	p. ____

Parts of the Body	Music Terms	Boat Terms

Experts of the Dictionary
Expert

Name _____

Find each word in the dictionary and write the page where you found the word. Then decide whether your word is a bird, an animal, or a tool. Write the word in the correct category below.

1. sloth   p._____   8. wren   p. ____   15. kudu   p. ____
2. petrel   p. ____   9. tanager   p. ____   16. scythe   p. ____
3. hod   p. ____   10. wombat   p. ____   17. grouse   p. ____
4. emu   p. ____   11. peccary p. ____   18. ibex   p. ____
5. lemur   p. ____   12. shrike   p. ____   19. awl   p. ____
6. plumb   p. ____   13. trowel   p. ____   20. skua   p. ____
7. winch   p. ____   14. osprey   p. ____   21. gimlet   p. ____

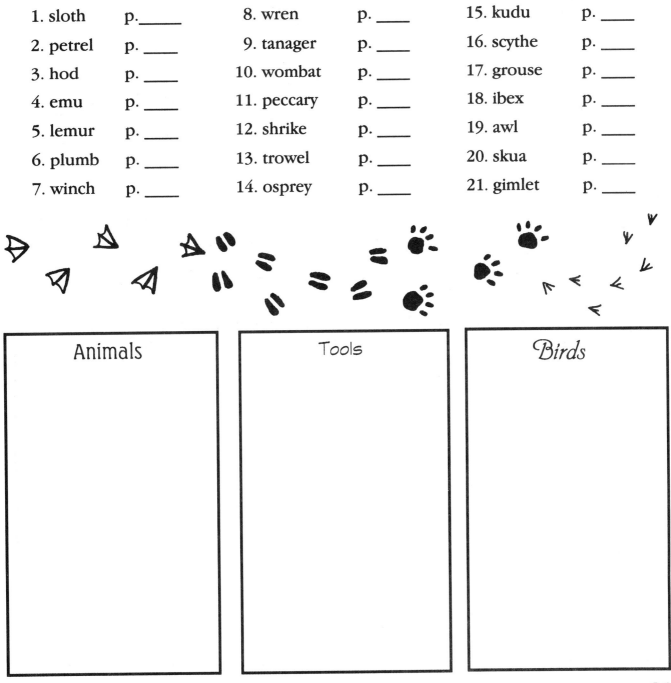

Animals	Tools	Birds

- *The best things I did this summer*
- *This year I hope to learn about . . . because . . .*
- *Some of the things I enjoy doing with my family*
- *My most serious accident*
- *My best memory of last year's class*
- *The rules all students should follow at school*
- *This year I think I'm going to like . . . because . . . I'm not sure I'm going to like . . . because . . .*
- *My favorite type of music is . . . because . . .*
- *The pet in my life (If you don't have a pet, describe one you'd like to have.)*
- *My favorite sport is . . . because . . .*

Poems to Memorize

2nd grade: "The Sun and Moon" by Elaine Laron. This is a lovely poem from the book *Free to be You and Me,* Bantam Books, where the author tells the reader that she would rather shine on her own than reflect someone else's light.

3rd grade: "Surprise" by Beverly McLoughland, *Good Books, Good Times!,* selected by Lee Bennett Hopkins, Harper & Row. This is a short poem that shows us that authors often know about us without knowing us.

4th grade: "On a Day in Summer" by Aileen Fisher, from *Good Books, Good Times!,* selected by Lee Bennett Hopkins, Harper & Row. At a time when summer is still fresh on our minds, this is a wonderful poem to remind us that books and summer go well together.

5th grade: "I'd Like a Story" by X. J. Kennedy, from *Good Books, Good Times!,* selected by Lee Bennett Hopkins, Harper & Row. This is a book about books and imagination.

6th grade: same as 5th grade.

Note some of your special poems for memorization

Poems to Write

Getting Started

Once or twice a month students should have the opportunity to write poetry. Many teachers are hesitant to teach poetry writing because they aren't certain that they are doing it correctly. If the students are developing as skillful writers, you're probably doing it right. Besides, the poetry police are not going to come to your room to check on you. Just enjoy it. First, remind students that poetry does not have to rhyme to be poetry. Second, poetry is condensed writing. All of the unimportant words have been removed and only the most important words are left. The other thing to discuss is that poetry is descriptive and usually evokes images of things seen, tasted, smelled, heard, or felt. It takes a careful selection of words to create the image you want the reader to experience.

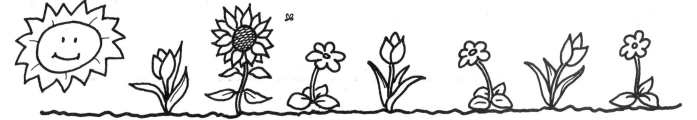

Two-Word Poems

The two-word poem is ideal to use for September with any grade. This poem is a wonderful start for students. It never fails to sound like a poem, and it makes the student immediately feel successful. The best way to do this is to work together on a subject. A fun one to start with is ice cream. The following example shows you how easy it is to write this type of poem.

Ice Cream
sticky stuff
tastes good
my favorite
chocolate fudge
with cone
hot summer
melting fast
yum yum

The only rules are that the poem must be about eight lines long and can only have two words per line. Any longer than eight lines or so and it stops sounding like a poem and starts sounding like a list. If it is any shorter, it does not sufficiently describe the subject. Do a sample poem together first by asking students to suggest two words at a time that can be associated with ice cream or that describe ice cream. On the left is a sample of what a class might write together on the board

Because it is only eight lines long, only eight students got a chance to contribute to this poem. After checking the group poem to see if this is the order that is best for the poem or if any lines should be moved around, you'll find that students will be anxious to try to write their own poems. At this point have them choose a favorite flavor of ice cream to write about. If it has only one word, such as "vanilla," they'll need to add another word such as "creamy" to make it "creamy vanilla." If it has three words such as "jamoca almond fudge," they will need to take away one word or add another word so that it will turn into two lines.

Other successful versions of this poem involve having students write about themselves, a friend, a book, a season, a favorite food, or a color. Almost any subject works well. This is a wonderful, highly successful way to start students' poetry careers in your classroom!

uni - one

unicycle: a riding device that has only one wheel and pedals like a bicycle

uniform: always the same; never changing; special clothes worn by the members of a certain group

unanimous: having one opinion held by all

unify: to make into one; unite

unicorn: an imaginary animal like a horse with one long horn in the center of its forehead

unique: that is the only one; there is nothing like it

unison: sameness of musical pitch

unite: to join together in one

university: an institution of learning whose program includes all branches of knowledge

bi - two

biannual: coming twice a year

bicuspid: a tooth with two points on its top surface

bicycle: a vehicle to ride on that has two wheels

biennial: happening once every two years/ lasting for two years

bilateral: having two sides

bimonthly: once every two months

binary: made up of two parts

bisect: to cut into two equal parts or to cut into two parts

tri - having three

triad: a group of three

triangle: a flat figure with three sides and three angles

triathlon: a contest that tests the ability of athletes in three events (swimming, bicycling, and running) without a break

tricycle: a vehicle for children to ride on that has three wheels

trident: a spear with three prongs

trilogy: a set of three plays, novels, etc.

trio: a piece of music for three voices or instruments/ any group of three

triple: made up of three/ three times as much

triplet: any of three children born at a single birth

tripod: a stand, frame, etc. with three legs

trisect: to divide into three parts

trivet: a small stand with three legs

Primary

- October is the tenth month of the year. Its name comes from the Latin word *octo*, meaning "eighth." Julius Caesar changed the calendar to make the year begin on January 1 instead of March 1.

- October has thirty-one days. The October flower is the marigold, and the birthstone is the opal.

- The week that includes October 8 is Fire Prevention Week.

1. This is the birthday of Jimmy Carter. He was the thirty-ninth president of the United States.

1. Colorado became the thirty-eighth state on this day in 1876.

3. On this day in 1950 the first "Peanuts" comic strip was published. "Peanuts" has Charlie Brown, Lucy, and Snoopy in it.

4. The first man-made satellite was launched by the U.S.S.R. in 1957. It was called <u>Sputnik</u>.

5. President Harry Truman was the first president to broadcast on television. It was on this day in 1947.

6. This is Universal Children's Day.

6. George Westinghouse was born on this day in 1846. He was an American inventor.

8. Jesse Jackson was born on this day in 1941. He is an American religious and political leader.

9. Leif Ericson landed in North America in about 1000 A.D.

10. Children's author James Marshall was born on this day.

11. This is the birthday of children's author Russell Freeman.

12. This is Columbus Day. In 1492 Christopher Columbus and his ships landed on the island of San Salvador.

14. On this day in 1744 the Earl of Sandwich created the world's first sandwich.

15. This is World Poetry Day.

16. This is the birth date of Noah Webster. He spent twenty years writing <u>An American Dictionary of the English Language</u>.

17. This is Black Poetry Day. Find out about Langston Hughes, Alice Walker, and Gwendolyn Brooks.

17. Millions of Americans watched the 1989 San Francisco earthquake on television while tuning in for the third game of the World Series.

18. The Statue of Liberty, a gift from France, was dedicated by President Cleveland on this date.

19. Thomas Edison began his first successful demonstration of the electric light on this day in 1879.

21. Alfred Nobel was born on this day in 1833. His will provides funds for Nobel Prizes.

24. This is United Nations Day.

26. This is the birthday of Richard Byrd. He was an American polar explorer.

26. This is the birthday of children's author Steven Kellogg.

28. Dr. Jonas Salk was born on October 28, 1914. He developed the Salk vaccine for polio.

31. Nevada became the thirty-sixth state on this day in 1864.

31. This is Halloween. Many people enjoy dressing in costumes on this day.

Upper Grades

- October is the tenth month of the year. Its name comes from the Latin word *octo,* meaning "eighth." Julius Caesar changed the calendar to make the year begin on January 1 instead of March 1.
- October has thirty-one days. The October flower is the marigold, and the birthstone is the opal.
- The week that includes October 8 is Fire Prevention Week.
- The second Monday in October is Canadian Thanksgiving.

1. Jimmy Carter, thirty-ninth president of the United States, was born on this day in 1924 in Plains, Georgia. President Carter worked hard for human rights, both at home and in other countries.

1. The United States gave back to Panama control of the Canal Zone in 1979.

2. Mohandas Gandhi, famous Indian political leader, was born on this day in 1869. Gandhi urged his followers to boycott anything English because the English ruled India. His nonviolent resistance served as a model for social change to many people around the world, including Dr. Martin Luther King, Jr.

3. On this day in 1950 the first "Peanuts" comic strip was published. Its creator was Charles Schulz. Snoopy, Charlie Brown, and Lucy are some of the "Peanuts" characters.

4. Sputnik 1, the first man-made earth satellite, was sent from Russia into orbit on this day in 1957.

4. This is the birth date of Rutherford B. Hayes, nineteenth president of the United States. He was born in 1822. He won over Samuel J. Tilden although Tilden had more popular votes than Hayes.

4. This is the birthday of Donald Sobol, author of the children's book Encyclopedia Brown.

5. Chester A. Arthur, twenty-first president of the United States, was born on this day in 1830. He became president when James Garfield died, seven months after being shot by an assassin.

5. This is the birthday of Louise Fitzhugh, author of Harriet the Spy, a book written for upper elementary boys and girls.

5. On this day in 1947 President Harry Truman became the first United States president to give a television speech.

6. George Westinghouse, American inventor and manufacturer, was born on this day in 1846.

6. The first talking movie, The Jazz Singer, was shown in New York on October 6, 1927.

6. This is the birth date of Thor Heyerdahl. Heyerdahl made a voyage of 4300 miles on the Kon-Tiki, a replica of an ancient sailing vessel.

8. The Great Chicago Fire started on this day in 1871. The fire destroyed 17,560 buildings in less than twenty-four hours.

8. On this date in 1956 Don Larsen pitched the first perfect no-hit, no-run, no-walk game in World Series history in New York City.

8. Reverend Jesse Jackson was born on this day in 1941. He is an American religious and political leader who works to achieve economic power for black Americans.

9. This is the birthday of American children's author Johanna Hurwitz.

9. This is the birthday of John Lennon, one of the former Beatles. He was born in 1940.

9. This day is Leif Ericson Day in honor of the Norseman who settled Greenland and traveled from Greenland to North America around the year 1000 A.D.

10. The ball-point pen was invented on this day by Lázió Biro.

10. On this day in 1887 everyone who lived on the South Atlantic island of Tristan da Cunha was evacuated after a volcano exploded.

10. Spiro Agnew resigned as vice-president of the United States on this day in 1973. He had been fined and put on probation for income tax evasion.

11. This is the birthday of Eleanor Roosevelt. She was first lady from 1933 to 1945. After her husband's death in 1945, President Truman appointed her as the United States' delegate to the United Nations.

11. On this day in 1886 the first patent for the adding machine was issued. It was invented by Dorr Eugene Felt of Chicago, Illinois.

12. This is Columbus Day. In 1492 Christopher Columbus and his ships landed on the island of San Salvador while looking for a shorter route to Asia.

13. Molly Pitcher, American Revolutionary War heroine, was born on this day in 1744. Although her real name was Molly Ludwig, she was called Molly Pitcher because on one of the hottest days of the war she carried water in a pitcher to thirsty soldiers on the battlefield. During the fighting her husband fell from a heat stroke. She took his place and fought the rest of the battle.

14. Dwight Eisenhower was the thirty-fourth president of the United States. He was born on this day in 1890 in Denison, Texas. Before he was president, he was commander of all the Allied forces in Europe during World War II.

14. The first person to break the sound barrier was Captain Charles Yeager of the United States Air Force. He did this on this date in 1947.

14. William Penn was born on this day in 1644. He was the founder of the Pennsylvania Colony. Penn named the area Sylvania, meaning "woods," because of its immense forests.

14. In 1744 the Earl of Sandwich created the world's first sandwich.

15. This is World Poetry Day.

16. Noah Webster was born on this day. In 1828 his American Dictionary of the English Language was published. It had taken him twenty years to complete.

17. This is Black Poetry Day. Find out about Langston Hughes, Alice Walker, and Gwendolyn Brooks.

17. Millions of Americans watched the 1989 San Francisco Earthquake on television while tuning in for the third game of the World Series.

18. The Statue of Liberty, a gift from France, was dedicated by President Grover Cleveland on this date in 1886.

19. In 1781 General Cornwallis surrendered to Washington at Yorktown, ending the American Revolutionary War.

19. On this day in 1752 Benjamin Franklin flew a homemade kite during a thunderstorm. When a bolt of lightning struck the kite and traveled down it to a key at the end of the kite, it proved that lightning is electricity.

21. Alfred Nobel, Swedish philanthropist and founder of the Nobel Prize, was born on this date in 1833. He is also famous for inventing and manufacturing dynamite.

21. Ferdinand Magellan entered the strait that now bears his name on this day in 1520.

22. On this day in 1797 Andre-Jacques Garnerin made the first successful parachute descent. He fell from a balloon at 2200 feet over Paris.

23. On this day in 1945 Jackie Robinson was signed by the Brooklyn Dodgers. He was the first black player to play for a major league team.

24. Sarah Hale was born on this day in 1788. She was an American writer who wrote "Mary Had a Little Lamb" and many other books, poems, and songs. She also worked hard to make Thanksgiving a national holiday.

25. Pablo Picasso was born on this day in 1881. He is famous for the many styles of his paintings. He lived in Spain and France.

26. On this day in 1825 the Erie Canal was opened to traffic. It is 350 miles long and links Lake Erie with the Hudson River.

27. Theodore Roosevelt, twenty-sixth president of the United States, was born on this day in 1858. He worked hard to save the natural resources of the country by establishing national parks and more than 125 million acres of national forests. The Teddy bear was named after him.

28. Dr. Jonas Salk, the American scientist who developed the Salk vaccine for polio, was born on this day in 1914.

29. On this day in 1929 the stock market collapsed, signaling the beginning of the Great Depression.

30. On this day in 1938 the radio play War of the Worlds, which was about an invasion from Mars, was broadcast. Although the station announced that it was just a play, panic was caused because people thought it was really happening.

30. This is the birthday of John Adams, second president of the United States. He was born in 1797 and was one of the writers of the Declaration of Independence.

31. Nevada became the thirty-sixth state on this day in 1864.

31. This day is Halloween. Its name came from "All Hallow's Eve," which marks the night before the Feast of All Saints. The ancient Druids celebrated New Year's Day on November 1. They believed that on New Year's Eve, October 31, the ghosts of the dead  were allowed to return to earth and visit their homes. Windows and doors were left open to welcome the good spirits. Large bonfires were lighted to scare off evil ghosts.

31. This is the birthday of Katherine Paterson, author of Bridge to Terabithia. She was born in China in 1932.

Descriptive Paragraphs

If there were only one technique to make students better writers, many teachers would choose this writing skill. With the teaching of descriptive writing, students not only become better writers, but more selective readers as well. Suddenly they see authors like Natalie Babbit, E. B. White, and Scott O'Dell as fine descriptive writers as well as good story tellers.

Reading Descriptive Writing

The students first need to understand how writers become illustrators with their words. Examples of this can be found in many paragraphs of *Charlotte's Web, Island of the Blue Dolphins, Homesick, My Own Story,* and *A Wrinkle in Time,* as well as many other finely written books. As you are reading with students, point out examples of good descriptive writing. Have them point out ways the author has used words and phrases to build images. Have them look for descriptive writing in their own reading.

Here are two descriptive paragraphs written by students. In addition to your examples from literature, these may be used as examples.

The pizza was hot. It was a great big pizza with lots of melted stringy cheese, but before the cheese there was a crisp crust. When you took a bite, it sizzled in your mouth. The cheese was terrific! The pizza had lots of crunchy bell peppers and tons of pepperoni that made your mouth water. The juicy olives were sliced in half so you could get one in every bite. The tangy mushrooms were sliced down to fourths. The sausage was crispy cooked to a dark brown, and to top it off, it made my mouth water.

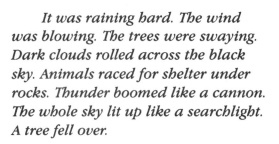

It was raining hard. The wind was blowing. The trees were swaying. Dark clouds rolled across the black sky. Animals raced for shelter under rocks. Thunder boomed like a cannon. The whole sky lit up like a searchlight. A tree fell over.

Discussion

After reading an example from a novel or one of the examples above, discuss our senses and ask if the paragraph that was read included references to one or more senses. Discuss the senses that were referenced. Ask how the author used words to show what he or she saw, felt, tasted, heard, or smelled.

After you have discussed one paragraph, move on to another. Ask the students why you might have chosen this one as an example, how the author created an image for you with his or her words, and what words or phrases were especially appealing to them.

It is important that students see how words can create pictures for the reader better than illustrations do. You might even ask your students why words are better in some ways than pictures.

Writing Descriptively

The next step, now that students understand the concept of "show me with your words," is to move on to the writing stage. Their first assignment is to describe a messy bedroom. Remind them that their writing is to be believable. They are to include as many senses as appropriate and remember that they are writing a paragraph, not a story. This last part is extremely important. Their paragraph will be written as if someone is standing in the doorway, looking across the room and describing what they are seeing.

Tell the students that you will be choosing the five to six most descriptive papers. These will be read aloud with the author's permission. Let them know that they have about twenty minutes for this assignment. It is a rough draft.

This assignment can be done just before recess so that those who wish to work a little longer may continue. Collect the work after about twenty minutes.

Sharing Exemplary Writing

That evening sort the papers into three piles in terms of their use of descriptive writing — *yes, maybe*, and *no*. You may wish to note in your grade book a rubric grade or an *above, at*, or *below grade level* grade.

If you have five or six "definitely yes" papers, read each one orally to the class the next day, and, when you finish reading, ask students to tell what was especially descriptive about each one. After a few individuals have shared what made a paper descriptive, ask if the author objects to being identified. Then look around the room for a head nodding. Those writers are usually so proud that they love having their name announced. Two things occur because of this. One is that the author feels absolutely terrific. You may be surprised at who the fine descriptive writers in your class are.

They are often different than the story tellers, good book report writers, and good report writers. They often have a creative and sly sense of humor that causes people to enjoy reading their work. The other thing that happens is that the rest of the class has had some good modeling done for them and are ready to write again. Those whose work was chosen as good examples are hoping to be chosen again. Those who weren't chosen, feel that the next time will be their turn.

More Writing

Now it's time to write again. Usually this assignment is effective about twice a week for two to three weeks. Here are some other successful topics for this writing project:

- The hamburger
- The ocean/lake on a very hot day
- The ocean/lake on a very cold day
- The best pizza I ever had
- The storm
- My favorite dessert

As teachers we need to understand that not every writing assignment is a complete report or story. The skills taught in some short assignments like this one are immensely valuable to the students' future writing abilities.

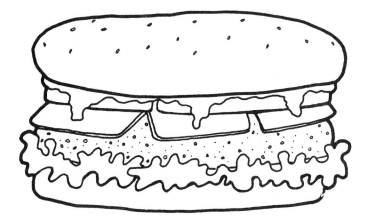

- *One of the best days of my life so far*
- *My ten favorite things in life (don't include people)*
  Rather than just listing things, encourage students to write varied sentences like "One of my favorite things in life is. . . because. . . Another thing I enjoy is . . . because. . . A third thing I love is . . . because. . ."
- *I get nervous when . . .*
- *Some of the things I'm good at*
- *A Halloween I remember*
- *My plans for this Halloween*
- *What I like best about school*
- *Some of the things I don't like (don't include people). . .*
- *My favorite breakfast. Use lots of adjectives. Make us hungry.*
- *The best way to enjoy a rainy day is . . .*
- *If I could change one rule at school*

Poems to Memorize

2nd grade: "Keep a Poem in Your Pocket" by Beatrice Schenk de Regniers, *Random House Book of Poetry*. This may initially look long to children with its three stanzas, but the rhyme of it and the repetition make it fairly easy to memorize. It is a sweet poem about how memorizing poetry can keep you from being lonely.

3rd grade: "Autumn Leaves" by Aileen Fisher, *Tomie de Paola's Book of Poems*, G. P. Putnam's Sons Sons, is a perfect poem for the change of seasons.

4th grade: "The Quarrel" by Eleanor Farjeon, *Random House Book of Poetry*, is a poem that helps us remember that being right all the time isn't as important as friendship.

5th grade: "Ations" by Shel Silverstein from *A Light in the Attic*, Harper & Row, is a wonderful poem about the steps of friendship.

6th grade: same as 5th grade.

Note some of your special poems for memorization

———

———

———

———

Poems to Write

Senses of the Seasons (or Holidays)

The poetry lesson for this month can actually be used anytime during the year. The first step is to think of a season or holiday. You may wish to have the students write a poem about summer as a class so that they can do autumn or Halloween by themselves.

What Is Summer Like?

Using summer as the example, ask students first to think about the tastes of summer. Two that they may think of are strawberries and ice cream. When you ask them to combine these two tastes into a line, they will probably come up with "summer tastes like strawberries and ice cream" or "the taste of summer is straw-

berries and ice cream." Write this on the board, but ask them to expand it and then expand it again. It might then be "summer tastes like red, ripe yummy strawberries and creamy ice cream melting in the hot sun." This is what  you're looking for, a line that describes the tastes of summer.

Once they have written this first line as a class, write several other lines to describe the smell, sound, look and feel of summer, using the same technique of combining two things and adding words to describe the two things.

Independent Writing

The next step is to have students take out a pencil and paper and brainstorm ideas about the taste of Halloween or autumn individually, once again using the senses to write expansive, descriptive phrases.

After you feel that nearly everyone is finished with the taste, go on to the other senses. Ask them to think about,

- What it smells like
- What it sounds like
- What it looks like
- What it feels like

Students should produce a beautiful, long, descriptive poem. Have them illustrate their poems with a picture for a bulletin board or type the poem, illustrate it, and save it for a book of poetry to be presented to parents at the end of the year.

pre - before

prearrange: to arrange ahead of time

precaution: care taken ahead of time

precede: to go or come before in time, order, etc.

precocious: having or showing much more ability, knowledge, etc., than is usual at such a young age

preconceive: to form an idea or opinion ahead of time

predict: to tell what one thinks will happen in the future

preface: an introduction to a book, article, or speech

prefer: to like better; choose first

prefix: a syllable or group of syllables joined to the beginning of a word to change its meaning

prejudge: to judge in advance or before one knows enough to judge fairly

premier: chief official; first in importance

previous: happening before in time or order

preview: a viewing or showing ahead of time

prevent: to keep from happening

re - back or again

reassemble: to come or put together again

reassure: to remove the doubts and fears of; make feel secure again

rebound: to bounce back

rebuild: to build again

recall: to bring back to mind; remember

recant: to take back an opinion or belief

reclaim: to get back

recognize: to be aware of something or someone again

recoil: to jump or shrink back suddenly

reexamine: to examine again

reform: to form again

reimburse: to pay back money

repeat: to say over again

resell: to sell again

return: to come back

rewrite: to write again

Primary

- November is the eleventh month of the year. November comes from the Latin word *Novem,* which means "nine."
- November has thirty days. The November flower is the chrysanthemum, and the November birthstone is the topaz.
- Children's Book Week is celebrated during the month of November.
- In the United States, Election Day is the first Tuesday after the first Monday in November.

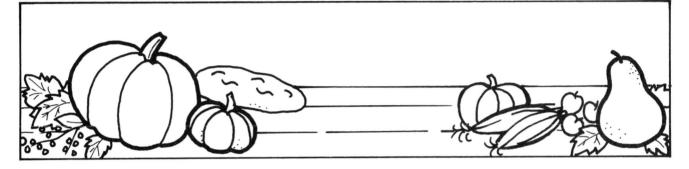

1. Author's Day is celebrated in November because so many famous authors have their birthdays this month.

2. Daniel Boone was a famous pioneer who explored what is now Kentucky. He was born in 1734.

2. North and South Dakota became states on November 2, 1889.

3. This is the birthday of an Englishman named John Montague. He was the Earl of Sandwich. He was born on November 3, 1718, and he invented the sandwich.

4. Will Rogers was born on this day. He was a famous American humorist and author.

5. In 1958 Shirley Chisholm became the first black woman to be elected to the U.S. House of Representatives.

6. This is the birth date of John Philip Sousa. He was born in 1854. He is famous for writing "Stars and Stripes Forever."

6. James Naismith was born on this day in 1861. He invented basketball using two peach baskets and a soccer ball.

7. Nobel winner Marie Curie was born on this day in 1867.

8. In 1889 Montana became the thirty-first state in the United States.

10. On this date in 1903 Mary Anderson was issued a patent for inventing the windshield wiper.

11. Washington became the forty-second state on November 11, 1889. Washington is the only state named for a president of the United States.

11. Veterans Day is a day set aside to honor those who have served their country.

12. Elizabeth Cady Stanton was born on November 12, 1815. She educated people about female voting rights.

13. Robert Louis Stevenson was born on this day in 1850. He was a famous poet and novelist. He wrote <u>Treasure Island</u>.

14. This is the birth date of Astrid Lindgren, author of <u>Pippi Longstocking.</u> It is also the birthday of William Steig, who wrote <u>Sylvester and the Magic Pebble.</u>

15. Schichi-go-san is celebrated today in Japan. Children visit shrines and offer gifts of thanksgiving.

16. Oklahoma became a state on this date in 1907. The state's name comes from the Choctaw Indian words that mean "red people."

17. The Suez Canal was opened on this day in 1869 in Egypt.

18. This is the birthday of Mickey Mouse. He appeared in the first talking movie cartoon, Steamboat Willie, in 1928.

19. This is the birth date of James Garfield. He was the twentieth president of the United States.

20. Children's author William Cole was born on this date.

20. The first child born in the American colonies of English parents was Peregrine White. She was born on this date in 1620.

21. On this date in 1620, the pilgrims signed their famous document called The Mayflower Compact. This was their first plan for governing themselves.

21. North Carolina became the twelfth state in 1789.

23. Franklin Pierce was our fourteenth president. He was born on this day in 1804.

24. Zachary Taylor was our twelfth president. He was born on this day in 1784.

24. This is the birthday of Carlo Collodi. He wrote Pinocchio.

25. Marc Brown was born on November 25, 1946. He wrote the Arthur series of books.

26. This is Sojourner Truth Memorial Day.

25. The fourth Thursday in November is Thanksgiving Day. President Lincoln proclaimed it a holiday in 1863.

28. The first post office in the United States opened on this date in 1783.

29. This is the birth date of Louisa May Alcott. She was the author of Little Women.

30. Mark Twain, the famous American author who wrote The Adventures of Tom Sawyer, was born on this day in 1835.

Upper Grades

- November is the eleventh month of the year. November comes from the Latin word *Novem,* which means "nine."
- November has thirty days. The November flower is the chrysanthemum, and the November birthstone is the topaz.
- Children's Book Week is celebrated during the month of November.
- In the United States, Election Day is the first Tuesday after the first Monday in November.

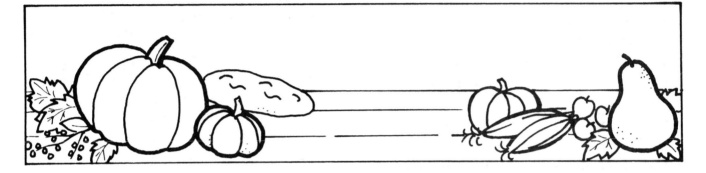

1. Author's Day has been celebrated on this day since 1938. Many famous authors were born in November. Among those who have November birthdays are Mark Twain, Louisa May Alcott, and Robert Louis Stevenson.

2. Daniel Boone was born on this day in 1734. He was a frontiersman who explored the unknown forests of Kentucky. Thousands of pioneers followed in his footsteps.

2. James Polk, the eleventh president of the United States, was born on this date in 1795. Polk tried to buy California from Mexico, but it wouldn't sell. He, therefore, forced Mexico into a war. As a part of the peace treaty, Polk bought five of our states from Mexico.

2. The twenty-ninth president of the United States, Warren G. Harding, was born on this date in 1865. Harding was president from 1921 to August 1923, when he died.

2. Both North and South Dakota were admitted to the Union as the thirty-ninth and fortieth states on this date in 1889.

3. This is the birthday of an Englishman named John Montague. He was the Earl of Sandwich. He was born on November 3, 1718. He invented the sandwich.

3. Bette Bao Lord wrote <u>Year of the Boar and Jackie Robinson</u>. She was born on November 3, 1938, in Shanghai, China.

4. Will Rogers, American humorist and author, was born on this day in 1879.

4. On this day in 1922 archaeologist Howard Carter discovered the steps leading to the tomb of Egyptian pharaoh Tutankhamon.

5. Guy Fawkes Day is celebrated on this day in Canada and Great Britain. Fawkes and a group of dissidents tried to blow up King James I and the Parliament on this date in 1605. The plot failed and Guy Fawkes Day is observed each November 5.

5. Shirley Chisholm became the first black woman to be elected to the U.S. House of Representatives. This happened in 1958.

6. John Philip Sousa was born on this date in 1854. He was famous for writing "Stars and Stripes Forever," as well as many other famous marches.

6. James Naismith invented the game of basketball in 1891. He wanted to create a game that could be played indoors during the winter. He used two peach baskets and a soccer ball for the first game. He was born on November 6, 1861.

7. Nobel physicist Marie Curie was born on this date in 1867.

8. Montana became the thirty-first state in 1889. Montana is the Spanish word for "mountain."

8. Franklin D. Roosevelt was elected president of the United States on this day in 1932. He was the only president to be elected four times. It is now the law that no one may be elected more than twice.

9. The Holocaust began on this date in 1938, when Nazi storm troopers burned synagogues and smashed Jewish shops in Germany. It is called Kristallnacht, meaning "night of shattered glass."

10. On this date in 1903 Mary Anderson was issued a patent for inventing the windshield wiper.

11. Washington became the forty-second state on this date in 1889. Washington is the only state named for a president of the United States.

11. Originally this date was called Armistice Day in honor of those who gave their lives in World War I. An armistice was signed on this date. Now this holiday is in honor of those who have served our country and it is called Veterans Day.

12. This is the birth date of Elizabeth Cady Stanton. Stanton was an American leader of women's suffrage who educated people about female voting rights. She was born on this day in 1815.

13. Scottish poet and novelist Robert Louis Stevenson was born on this day in 1850. He is famous for A Child's Garden of Verses and Treasure Island.

14. Robert Fulton was born on this day in 1765. He was an American inventor, civil engineer, and artist. He is best known for designing and building the Clermont, the first commercially successfully steamboat. It was originally called the North River Steamboat.

14. This is the birth date of Claude Monet, a French artist who is famous for his work with the effects of light and color in art. He was born in 1840.

14. Two famous children's authors were born on this date. Astrid Lindgren, author of Pippi Longstocking, and William Steig, who wrote Sylvester and the Magic Pebble, are the two authors.

15. Famous American painter Georgia O'Keeffe was born on this date in 1887. She is best known for her paintings of large flowers.

15. The Articles of Confederation were adopted by the Continental Congress in 1777.

16. Oklahoma became the forty-sixth state in 1907. The state's name comes from the Choctaw Indian words okla, for "people," and humma, for "red."

16. Jean Fritz, American children's author, was born on this day. One of her most popular books is Homesick, My Own Story. She is also well-known for her many biographies of famous Americans.

17. This is the anniversary of the opening of the Suez Canal in Egypt. It opened on November 17, 1869.

17. Explorers Lewis and Clark reached the Pacific Ocean on this date in 1805.

18. This is the birthday of Mickey Mouse. He appeared in the first talking movie cartoon, Steamboat Willie, in 1928.

18. U.S. sea captain Nathaniel Palmer discovered Antarctica on this date in 1820.

19. James Garfield, twentieth president of the United States, was born on this day in 1831. Garfield was shot and killed by a man to whom he had denied a job.

19. Abraham Lincoln delivered the Gettysburg Address on this date in 1863. Although the entire speech is only 300 words, it is one of the most famous speeches ever given.

21. Elizabeth Speare, author of The Witch of Blackbird Pond, was born on this date in 1928.

21. North Carolina became the twelfth state on this date in 1789.

22. On this date in 1963 President John F. Kennedy was assassinated in Dallas, Texas.

23. Franklin Pierce, fourteenth president, was born on this day in 1804. He won the Democratic nomination on the forty-ninth ballot as a compromise candidate.

24. On this day in 1642 the Dutch navigator Abel Tasman discovered Tasmania.

24. This is the birthday of Amelia Earhart. She was a famous American aviator. She was the first woman to cross the Atlantic alone in an airplane, to make a nonstop flight across the United States, and to fly from Hawaii to California. In 1937 her airplane disappeared in the South Pacific Ocean.

24. Zachary Taylor, twelfth president of the United States, was born on this date in 1784. Taylor had been an army general. He died only five days after becoming ill, having been in office only sixteen months.

24. This is the birthday of Carlo Lorenzini (known as Carlo Collodi), author of Pinocchio. This work started as a weekly serial for children, but eventually Pinocchio was made into a book.

26. Sojourner Truth Memorial Day is on this day in honor of black American abolitionists.

26. Charles Schulz, creator of the Peanuts comic strip, was born on this date.

26. The first national Thanksgiving Day in the United States was proclaimed by President George Washington in 1789. It became a  traditional holiday, held each year on the last Thursday in November, when Lincoln, proclaimed it an official national holiday in 1864. This was due to the efforts of Sarah Hale.

29. Three famous authors of books for young adults and adults were born on this date. Madeleine L'Engle, author of A Wrinkle in Time; C.S. Lewis, author of The Chronicles of Narnia; and Louisa May Alcott, author of Little Women, were all born on November 30.

29. Commander Richard E. Byrd and a crew of three were the first to fly over the South Pole on November 29, 1929.

30. Mark Twain, famous American author of The Adventures of Tom Sawyer and Huckleberry Finn, was born on this day in 1835. His real name was Samuel Langhorne Clemens.

30. This is the birth date of Jonathan Swift, author of Gulliver's Travels. He was born on this date in 1667.

Organized Paragraph Writing

November is a good time to begin working on writing descriptive paragraphs. In addition to writing descriptively, another writing skill students need is how to organize paragraphs with a main idea and appropriate details for nonfiction papers. One of the ways to accomplish both of these goals is with "organized paragraphs."

1. The first step is to think of a topic sentence to use as an example for your class to write about as a group. One I have used before is, *"(your town) is a great place to live."*

We then write two facts about why it is a great place to live. You should discuss several ideas. You might start the second sentence, "One of the reasons it's a great place to live is . . ." or "Many people think it's a great place to live because . . ." Remember to limit this second sentence to just one idea. Then move on to the second reason why your town is a good place to live.

Review potential beginnings for this second sentence. Some possible ones are, "Another reason people think it's a great place to live is . . ." or "A second reason . . ." You should then have a three-sentence paragraph on the board that may look something like this:

Santa Barbara is a great place to live. I think it's terrific because the climate is mild. Another reason I think it's great is that it has a wonderful area by the beach.

2. At this point you will have a topic sentence and two supporting sentences. The next step is to show the students how to expand the idea. We do this by erasing the last sentence to make room for a detail sentence that expands or explains the second sentence. In the case above, ask how the mild climate is terrific. The answer might be:

Santa Barbara is a great place to live. I think it's terrific because the climate is mild. The mild climate lets us enjoy outdoor activities like running, playing volleyball, rollerblading, and picnicking all year round.

3. Then add the next sentence, the one you had erased, and add a detail sentence to this sentence. The last job is to conclude, that is, to write a sentence that summarizes the paragraph. When finished, the paragraph has a topic sentence, two supporting sentences with detail sentences, and a conclusion. The finished paragraph looks like this.

Santa Barbara is a great place to live. I think it's terrific because the climate is mild. The mild climate lets us enjoy outdoor activities like running, playing volleyball, rollerblading, and picnicking all year round. Another reason I think it's great is that it has a wonderful area by the beach. On Sundays there is an art show there, bicycle riding, and people walking in the sunshine. Yes, Santa Barbara is a great city in which to live.

4. After working on this paragraph together, the students could be given the following topic sentence: "(fill in with a friend's name) is a good friend to have." After everyone has written this on his or her paper, have them write a supporting sentence.

After everyone is finished, have a few people read their sentences aloud. This helps others to know if they are on the right track. Then ask students who shared their sentences to give a detail sentence. You also might want to provide an example by choosing a child from the class (maybe one that no one else would choose) and give the topic sentence, the supporting sentence, and the detail sentence as an example. After the examples have been read (students' and/or yours), students then write detail sentences, and you again ask for volunteers to read their work.

When you feel that everyone is ready, have them write the last supporting sentence, the detail sentence, and the concluding sentence. Even though the process moves very slowly at this point, it guarantees that everyone understands the concept. Moving slowly beats reteaching every time!

5. What next? The next day work on a topic sentence that pertains to the social studies or science unit you are studying. A second grade class might by studying community helpers and have this sentence:

Fire fighters help our community.

A fifth grade class might be studying the colonies and have this sentence:

There were three major crops in the Southern Colonies.

If you feel your class is ready for a third supporting sentence and its detail sentence, this would be an opportunity to extend the writing assignment to three instead of two sentences.

Additional Considerations

If you teach this organizational tool to students as a whole, you will find that it carries over into their nonfiction writing. For some students it is the "Oh, I get it!" realization. For further practice, remember to:

- Choose various topics from your social studies, science, literature, and math units. You can also use sports, holidays, favorite fruits, favorite authors, and hobbies.

- Work on this about twice a week for three weeks for good understanding on the students' part.

- Let students know that all paragraphs don't need concluding sentences.

- If everyone understands the concept well, begin to add the idea of sentence variation.

- Teach students to vary their transitions.

First Report

By November you should have students begin their first research reports. This project involves research and organization as well as writing skills. Before the report is started, it is important that parents are notified. This may be done with a letter that requires a signature indicating that they are aware of this report. Let them know when the report is due, how much will be done in class, and what is required.

Here is a sample letter:

---

date

Dear Parents,

This is a letter to let you know that we are beginning work on a report about _____. It will be due on _____. It is to be (typed, handwritten, etc.). Your child has a copy of the report form that explains what is to be on each page of the report. He/She also has a point sheet that will be attached to the report after the cover page. Please look over these two papers with your child. The point page will require your signature to show that you have looked over the report and have made suggestions when the report is completed. We will work on this for _____ days in class until (date) and the rest will be done at home. Thank you for your assistance.

Please sign on the line below to indicate that you are aware of this report and the due date.

Sincerely,

your name

_____

parent's signature

The students should then be given a report form and a point page (example follows). Starting in fourth grade, they should also be given a sample of a Works Cited page. The advantage in clarifying what is on each page of the report is that you can specify information that the students have been studying. It also discourages copying because the information in most books is not presented in the same order. This also breaks up the report into small enough pieces so the students are not so overwhelmed. Too, it gives the parents information about how they need to assist at home. Students should also be taught about plagiarizing others' work. It is illegal and it is wrong. Included in this book are some examples of a report form and a point page.

It is important, too, that the students know what is acceptable to retrieve from the computer and what is not. It is easy these days to have complete reports with maps and artwork taken directly off the computer and printed. As a teacher, you need to decide and specify what is acceptable.

Step 1 - Graphic Organization

After a topic has been chosen, the first thing students need to do is brainstorm ideas related to this topic. This can be done many ways. Clustering or webbing, listing, note cards, or outlining are among many ways students may start. If, for instance, the students are going to write about emperor penguins, here are four ways they might organize their information.

The first technique is **webbing** or **clustering**. To organize in this manner, students write the topic in a circle in the middle of a piece of paper. They then think of concepts that are related to this topic and write them in circles that radiate from the main topic. Ideas that are related to these subtopics are attached to the appropriate circle. When students have finished mapping out all the possible related subtopics, they can then choose which ones they will include in their reports and organize these into a coherent article. An example is shown at the bottom of this page.

A second way to organize is with **note cards**. Students put a category on each card and fill the card with information about that category. Another way to use note cards is to record notes from reference material, switching to a new card whenever a new topic or fact is encountered. Then organize cards so that all the information about one topic is together, all the information about another topic is together, and so on. This allows students to get information from several different sources and integrate it into one organized format.

Brainstorming is a technique that is best used at the beginning of a report-writing project. It is a way to list information randomly, letting one idea spark several other, perhaps unrelated, ideas. To use this technique students would list ideas that are related to their report topic on one sheet of paper. These could be ideas about things to include in the report, questions that need to be answered, or points that need to be researched. When the list is finished, students then group these ideas into categories, fill in any missing parts with additional research, and write their reports.

Outlining is a method that is often used in grades above fourth, although with other methods becoming more popular, it is being used less and less. It is an effective method, however, to show the varying levels of importance of material or to demonstrate how facts and details elaborate a main idea. For students to effectively use this method, they will need some guided practice first. Select a section from your social studies text and as a group develop an outline that shows the main ideas and supporting ideas. Then as a group take a topic like "Caring for Your Dog" or "Planning a Vacation" and develop an outline that includes at least three main ideas and several supporting details.

Teaching students various ways of organizing materials helps them have more choices in finding what works best for them.

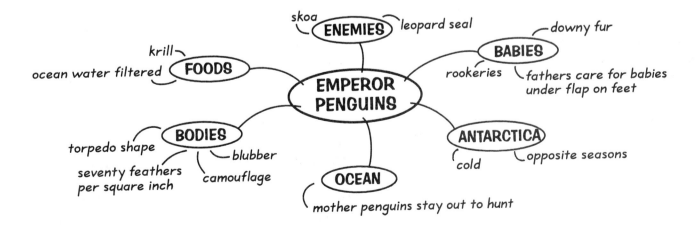

Step 2 - Begin

The second step is to have students begin their reports in class. They may wish to start immediately on the cover page, or they can save that for later. The main thing is for the students to start working on some aspect of their reports; for them to "buy into the project." Once they have completed a page or two, they find that the task is a completable one. Usually, having them work for one week in class and then complete the assignment at home works best, but each class is different and each report is different.

Usually students need about three to five weeks to do a good job on reports. It's a good idea to check every two days to see how much has been completed. If anyone turns in a report early, look it over and if it looks good, with the author's permission, show it page by page to the class. If you are able to keep one or two from previous-year students, these are good to model.

Samples

On the following five pages are examples of two reports (one on an animal and one on a country) as well as a works cited example that might be used starting at fourth grade level.

Animal Report

This report is due on_____at___o'clock. If it is not turned in at this time, it will be considered late and points will be subtracted. Remember to write your report in your own words. The report should contain the following information.

Cover Page

This is to have the name of your animal at the top, a large picture of your animal in the center, and your name at the bottom. Use unlined paper.

Information Pages

Paragraph 1 - Where It Lives

This paragraph is to tell the countries (territories, states, etc.) in which your animal is found and the type of land (marshy, desert, mountainous, etc.) on which it lives.

Paragraph 2 - What It Looks Like

This paragraph is to describe your animal's body. You are to include size, colors, weight ranges as an adult, and skin texture.

Paragraph 3 - About Its Young

Paragraph three is to tell about the young - what they are called, how they look, how they are cared for, and how they are fed.

Paragraph 4 - Its Enemies

This paragraph is to tell about your animal's enemies and how it protects itself.

Paragraph 5 - What It Eats

This paragraph is to tell what it eats and how it obtains its food.

Paragraph 6 - Other Facts

Paragraph six is to include any other facts you have learned that are not mentioned above but are interesting and/or important.

Paragraph 7 - Conclusion

This paragraph is your conclusion. It is to tell about your animal's importance to the environment and to summarize what you have learned.

Works Cited

See Guidelines for Works Cited for more information.

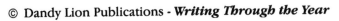

Point Sheet for Animal Report

Name_____   Date_____

Report on_____

Attach this page after the cover page and before the written pages.

	Points earned	Possible Points	Criteria
Cover page	_____	10	neatly done according to directions
Information pages	_____	10	spelling
	_____	10	neatness
	_____	10	punctuation
	_____	5	margins and indentations
	_____	40	quality of material and writing style
	_____	5	parent's signature
Works cited page	_____	10	done according to directions
Total	_____	**100**	

I have read my child's report and have made suggestions.

_____
Parent's signature

COUNTRY REPORT

This report is due on_____at___o'clock. If it is not turned in at this time, it will be considered late and points will be subtracted. Remember to write your report in your own words. The report should contain the following information.

Cover Page

This is to have the name of your country at the top, a very large flag of the country in the center, and your name at the bottom. Use unlined paper.

Map Page

Using unlined paper draw a map of the country, including major cities, land features, and rivers.

Facts Page

This page should be a chart that includes the capital, official language, area, elevation, population, and currency.

Information Pages

Paragraph 1 - Natural Resources

Start with an especially interesting fact about the natural resources (minerals, forests, farm land) of the country. Then tell about these resources.

Paragraph 2 - Diet

In this paragraph tell about the food people eat on a regular basis and what is eaten on special occasions.

Paragraph 3 - Educational System

Describe the educational system of the country. Answer questions such as, "Who goes to school?" "Is education required?" "What percentage of people go to high school and college?"

Paragraph 4 - Religion

Describe the religious makeup of the country. Does religion play an important part in the laws and behavior of the people? If so, how?

Paragraph 5 - History

In paragraph form, describe five important events in the history of the country.

Paragraph 6 - Government

Tell about the type of government this country has.

Paragraph 7 - Conclusion

In the concluding paragraph, tell what you found most interesting about this country and what you would like to see and do if you visited there.

Works Cited

See Guidelines for Works Cited for more information.

Point Sheet for COUNTRY REPORT

Your Name _____   Due Date _____

Report on _____

Attach this page after the cover page and before the written pages.

	Points earned	Possible Points	Criteria
Cover page	_____	5	neatly done according to directions
Map page	_____	10	neatly done, all features labeled
Facts page	_____	10	neatly done, accurate facts
Information pages	_____	10	spelling
	_____	10	neatness
	_____	10	punctuation
	_____	5	margins and indentations
	_____	25	quality of material and writing style
	_____	5	parent's signature
Works cited page	_____	10	done according to directions
Total	_____	100	

I have read my child's report and have made suggestions.

_____

Parent's signature

Guidelines for Works Cited

The purpose of a works cited page is to identify all your sources of information in one alphabetical list. Each entry should include all information required to identify a source. Here are examples of how to write the entries for your works cited. You should list all of your sources of information. They should be listed alphabetically according to the author's last name. When a listing is more than one line long, all lines after the first line should be indented. If the name of the author is not given in the article or book, begin the listing with the title of the article or book.

1. **Book with one author**

   Caney, Steven. <u>Invention Book</u>. New York: Workman Publishing, 1985.

2. **Book with more than one author**

   Barker, Joyce and George Johnson. <u>All About Hurricanes</u>. Johnstown, PA: Academic Press, 1989.

3. **An article in an encyclopedia**

   Chapin, Edward. "Millipede," <u>The World Book Encyclopedia</u>. Chicago: Field Enterprises, 1973, vol. 15, pp. 104-105.

4. **A newspaper article**

   Karr, Albert. "OSHA Sets Rules for Vehicles," <u>Wall Street Journal</u>. July 8, 1990, p. A-8.

5. **A magazine article**

   Powell, Bill. "A Truce in the Trade Wars." <u>Newsweek</u>. 34: 95-96, July 19, 1990.

6. **An Interview**

   Allen, Jill, county personnel director. Interviewed on July 12, 1990.

7. **Television show**

   NBC, "Nova: Genes," October 14, 1990.

8. **Unpublished works**

   Dees, John. "How to Train a Dog." 1989.

9. **Letter**

   Braggett, Jan, scientist with Dacon Industries, letter dated July 6, 1990.

10. **Information retrieved from the computer**

    "Centipede and Millipede," <u>Compton's New Century Encyclopedia</u>, CD edition, ver. 4.0, 1995.

    Zoroya, Gregg. "The Fisherman," July 13, 1997. Http://www.latimes.com.

- *Some of the good things that have happened to me are . . .*
- *When school is out today . . .*
- *It's not fair when . . .*
- *The most interesting animal to me is . . . because . . .*
- *Tell me about your best friend so that I would like him or her too*
- *A Thanksgiving I remember*
- *On this Thanksgiving my plans are . . .*
- *If I had a time machine I would . . .*
- *The time I felt like a real turkey (Explain that sometimes we all do something that makes us feel foolish. What happened?)*
- *I am grateful for . . .*

Poems to Memorize

2nd grade: An Arnold Lobel poem about books that begins with the line, "Books to the Ceiling," from *Once Upon a Time*, G. P. Putnam's Sons.

3rd grade: "Being Lost" by Karla Kuskin is a poem about getting lost in a book, from *Good Times, Good Books!* selected by Lee Bennett Hopkins, Harper & Row.

4th grade: "There is a Land," by Leland B. Jacobs, is a delightful poem about all that you can find by reading. This is from *Good Times, Good Books!* selected by Lee Bennett Hopkins, Harper & Row.

5th grade: "The Library," by Barbara A. Huff, is a poem about the magic of reading. This is from *Random House Book of Poetry*, Random House.

6th grade: same as 5th grade.

Note your special poems for memorization

———————————————————————————————

———————————————————————————————

———————————————————————————————

Poems to Write

Diamante

A diamante is a wonderful poem for this month because it concentrates on descriptive words. Its form is simple when you work from both directions to the middle. For younger students, this may be done as a class lesson. The structure of the poem is:

- The title is the topic.
- The next line contains two adjectives.
- The next line contains three action words.
- The fourth line contains four nouns or a phrase, changing topics (see sample).
- The fifth line contains three action words about the new subject.
- The sixth line contains two adjectives about the new subject.
- The last line contains the new topic that is the opposite of the first topic.

Puppy
puppy
exuberant, cuddly
chewing, running, yipping
growing larger, slowing down
eating, walking, barking
loyal, content
dog

The students will be able to list many opposites, and this is a good thing to do before they start. Here are some that are successful:

- day - night
- spring - fall
- summer - winter
- rain - sunshine
- young - old

Concrete Poems

Concrete poetry is a fun activity for any grade. The object is to write a poem and then use the words to outline a picture of the subject. It helps if students make a light outline to write on and then erase the outline after the poem has been written in the correct shape.

Here are some examples.

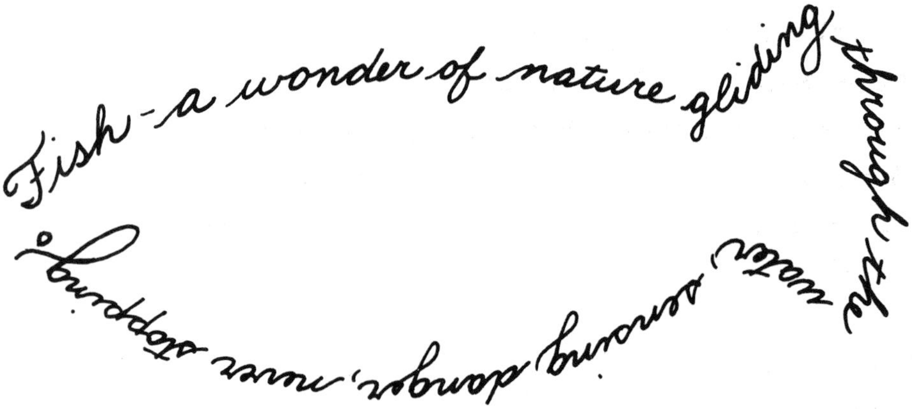

sub - below

sub-freezing: below freezing

submarine: a kind of warship that can travel under the surface of water

submerge: to put, go, or stay under water

subsequent: coming after

subterranean: underground

subway: an underground railway

therm/thermo - having to do with heat

thermal: having to do with heat

thermometer: a device for measuring temperature

thermos: a container for keeping liquids at almost the same temperature for several hours

thermostat: a device for operating a heating or cooling system that maintains an even temperature.

less - without

careless: without care

friendless: without friends; alone

fearless: without fear

hopeless: without expectation or hope

restless: without rest; uneasy

sleepless: without sleep; always awake

tireless: without getting tired; never weary

Primary

- December is the twelfth month of the year. December comes from the Latin word *decem*, meaning "ten." December once had twenty-nine days, but Julius Caesar added two more.
- The December flower is the narcissus, although holly and poinsettia are also used. The birthstone is turquoise or zircon.
- Hanukkah is the Jewish Feast of Lights. It begins on the eve of the twenty-fifth day of the Hebrew month of Kislev and lasts eight days. It usually falls in the month of December.

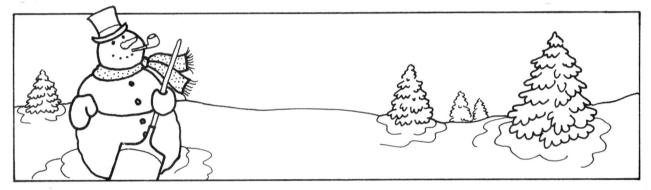

1. This is the birthday of children's author Jan Brett. She wrote <u>The Trouble With Trolls</u> and <u>Berlioz the Bear.</u> Jan Brett was born on December 1, 1949.

2. This is the birthday of author David Macaulay. He is famous for his amazing books. One of his books is about castles.

3. The planet Uranus was discovered on this day in 1781 by English astronomer William Herschel.

3. Illinois became the twenty-first state on this date in 1818.

5. Walt Disney was born on December 5, 1901. He is famous for his many cartoon characters and theme parks.

6. Families in Europe celebrate the Feast of St. Nicholas on this day.

7. Delaware became the first U.S. state in 1787 by ratifying the Constitution first.

7. On this day in 1941 Japanese planes bombed Pearl Harbor. The United States entered World War II on this day.

8. On this day in 1765 Eli Whitney was born. He was famous for inventing the cotton gin. Before a machine was invented, the work of separating cotton fibers from seeds was done slowly by hand.

9. On this day the first Christmas card was sent in England.

10. Mississippi became the twentieth state in 1817. It was named after the Mississippi River.

10. American poet Emily Dickinson was born on December 10, 1830. She wrote over 1600 poems.

11. Indiana became the nineteenth state on December 11, 1816.

11. UNICEF was established on this day in 1946.

12. Pennsylvania was the second state to ratify the Constitution, making it the second state in the United States.

12. On this date in 1901 Guglielmo Marconi and his assistant successfully transmitted the first radio signal across the Atlantic Ocean from England to Newfoundland.

13. New Zealand was discovered by Dutch explorer Abel Tasman on this date in 1642.

13. People in Sweden celebrate Santa Lucia's Day on this day with candlelight parades. This festival of light celebrates the return of more daylight hours.

14. On this day in 1911 a Norwegian expedition led by Roald Amundsen reached the South Pole.

14. Alabama became the twenty-second state on this date in 1819.

16. This is the birth date of Ludwig van Beethoven. Students may be familiar with his famous "Ode to Joy." He was born in 1770.

17. Orville and Wilbur Wright made the first successful airplane flight in 1903 in Kitty Hawk, North Carolina.

18. On this date in 1936 the first giant panda arrived in the United States from China.

18. New Jersey became the third state to join the United States.

20. On this date in 1803 the United States purchased almost a million square miles of territory from France.

21. The Pilgrims landed in Massachusetts, on this day in 1620.

21. Winter officially begins in the Northern Hemisphere on this day.

23. The Voyager made the first nonstop flight around the world without refueling on this day in 1986.

24. "Silent Night" was first sung on this day in 1818 in a village in Austria.

25. Christmas is celebrated in many countries on this date.

25. This is the birthday of Clara Barton, who founded the American Red Cross. She was born in 1821.

27. Louis Pasteur was a French scientist who was born on December 27, 1822. His discoveries led to the use of immunization to wipe out many diseases.

28. Iowa became the twenty-ninth state in 1846.

28. Woodrow Wilson was born on this date in 1856. He was the twenty-eighth president of the United States.

28. Chewing gum was first patented by William Sample on this day in 1869.

29. Texas became the twenty-eighth state in 1845.

29. Andrew Johnson was the seventeenth U.S. president. He was born on this date in 1808.

30. This is the birth date of Rudyard Kipling. He is most famous for The Jungle Book. He was born in 1865.

30. Children's author Mercer Mayer was born on this day in 1942.

31. In 1891 Ellis Island in New York Harbor was opened to receive immigrants to the United States.

Upper Grades

- December is the twelfth month of the year. December comes from the Latin word *decem*, meaning "ten." December once had twenty-nine days, but Julius Caesar added two more.
- The December flower is the narcissus, although holly and poinsettia are also used.
- The birthstone for this month is turquoise or zircon.
- Hanukkah is the Jewish Feast of Lights. It begins on the eve of the twenty-fifth day of the Hebrew month of Kislev and lasts eight days. It usually falls in the month of December.

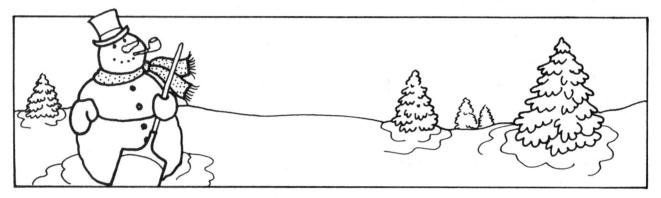

1. On this date Rosa Parks began the U.S. civil rights movement by refusing to give up her bus seat. This happened in Montgomery, Alabama, on December 1, 1955. Her arrest sparked the boycott of buses.

1. The first drive-in automobile service station was opened on this date in 1913. Gulf Refining Company opened it in Pittsburgh, Pennsylvania.

1. On this date in 1917 Father Edward Flanagan founded Boys Town, a community that offered shelter for homeless boys.

2. This is the birthday of author David Macaulay. He has written many interesting books, including <u>The Way Things Work</u> and <u>Castles.</u>

3. The planet Uranus was discovered on this day in 1781 by English astronomer William Herschel.

3. Illinois became the twenty-first state on this date in 1818.

5. The first football game in which the players wore numerals on their uniforms was played at the University of Pittsburgh on this day in 1908.

5. This is the birth date of Martin Van Buren, eighth president of the United States. He was born in 1782.

5. On this date in 1901 the creator of Disneyland, Disney World, and many well-known cartoon characters was born. This is Walt Disney's birth date.

6. Today is the Feast of St. Nicholas. Many European countries celebrate this holiday.

7. On December 7, 1941, Japanese forces attacked Pearl Harbor and destroyed the military and naval base on Oahu in Hawaii. This sudden attack plunged the United States into World War II.

7. Delaware became the first U.S. state in 1787 by being the first to ratify the Constitution.

8. This is the birth date of Eli Whitney. Whitney was famous for inventing the cotton gin. Before the machine was invented, the work of separating cotton fibers from seeds was done slowly by hand.

9. The first Christmas card was sent in England on this date in 1842.

9. In 1907 the first Christmas Seals, designed by Emily Bissell, went on sale. The proceeds from the sale of Christmas Seals are used to help fight lung diseases.

10. The first Nobel prizes were distributed on December 10, 1901, on the anniversary of the death of Alfred Nobel in 1896.

10. Mississippi became the twentieth state in 1817. It was named after the Mississippi River.

10. This is the birth date of American poet Emily Dickinson. Dickinson was born in 1830. She is famous for her many poems about love and nature.

10. In 1903 Marie and Pierre Curie won the Nobel Prize for their study of radioactivity.

11. Indiana became the nineteenth state on December 11, 1816.

11. UNICEF was established on this day in 1946. The United Nations International Children's Emergency Fund helps children all over the world.

12. On this date in 1901 Guglielmo Marconi and his assistant successfully transmitted the first radio signal across the Atlantic Ocean from England to Newfoundland.

12. Pennsylvania became the second state in 1787.

13. People in Sweden celebrate Santa Lucia's Day on this day with candlelight parades. This festival of light celebrates the return of more daylight hours.

13. The island of New Zealand was discovered in 1642 by Dutch explorer Abel Tasman.

14. On this day in 1911 a Norwegian expedition led by Roald Amundsen reached the South Pole.

14. This is the birth date of Margaret Chase Smith. She was the first woman in the United States to serve in both the House of Representatives and the Senate.

14. Alabama became the twenty-second state on this date in 1819.

15. Today is Bill of Rights Day. In 1791 the first ten amendments to the Constitution became law.

16. This is the anniversary of the Boston Tea Party. It was held on December 16, 1773, when American colonists dumped tea in Boston Harbor.

16. This is the birth date of Ludwig van Beethoven. Students may be familiar with his famous "Ode to Joy." He was born in 1770.

17. On this day in 1903 the Wright brothers had their first successful flight at Kitty Hawk, North Carolina.

18. New Jersey became the third state to ratify the Constitution, making it the third state in the United States.

18. Tchaikovsky's famous ballet, The Nutcracker, was first performed in St. Petersburg, Russia on this date in 1892.

18. The Thirteenth Amendment was ratified as part of the U.S. Constitution on this date in 1865. This amendment put an end to slavery.

18. On this date in 1936 the first giant panda arrived in the United States from China.

19. In 1732 Benjamin Franklin started publication of Poor Richard's Almanac.

20. The United States purchased almost a million square miles of territory from France in 1803. It was called the Louisiana Purchase.

21. The Pilgrims landed in Massachusetts on this day in 1620.

21. Today is the birthday of Avi, writer of many wonderful books for children and young adults.

21. Today winter begins. The winter solstice is when the sun is farthest from the equator. In Latin sol is "sun," and sito is "stand still."

23. The Voyager made the first nonstop flight around the world without refueling on this day in 1986.

24. The most popular song on this day in 1949 was "Rudolph the Red Nosed Reindeer."

24. "Silent Night" was first sung on this day in 1818. It was performed in the village church in Oberndorf, Austria.

25. Christmas is celebrated in many countries on this date.

25. This is the birthday of Clara Barton. She was born in 1821. She founded the American Red Cross and was its president in 1881.

25. Isaac Newton, the English mathematician who discovered the laws of gravitation, was born on this day in 1642.

27. Louis Pasteur, the French chemist who developed the pasteurization process, was born on this day in 1822. His discoveries led to the use of immunization to wipe out many diseases and sterilization to prevent food spoilage.

28. Iowa became the twenty-ninth state in 1846.

28. This is the birth date of Woodrow Wilson, twenty-eighth president of the United States. He was born in 1856. Wilson worked hard to establish the United Nations. He was the only President with a Ph.D.

29. On this date in 1845 Texas became the twenty-eighth state.

29. Andrew Johnson, the seventeenth U.S. president, was born on this date in 1808. Johnson became president when Lincoln was killed. He had a difficult time because of the Civil War and was nearly impeached because of his problems with Congress.

30. On this day in 1853 the United States bought the Arizona and New Mexico territory from Mexico. This was called the Gadsden Purchase.

30. This is the birth date of Rudyard Kipling. He is most famous for The Jungle Book. Kipling was the first English winner of the Nobel Prize for Literature, receiving this award in 1907.

31. Ellis Island in New York Harbor was opened on this date in 1891 to receive immigrants to the United States.

Fiction Writing

Of all the different types of writing, fiction is the most difficult for many people. Remind students that all stories must have the following elements:

- The story is told in the first person, "I," or third person, "she" or "he." Don't mix the perspective.

- Show, don't tell. This is the skill students learned in October's descriptive writing lesson. Use descriptive writing in showing where and when the story is taking place, as well as in descriptions of the characters.

- What is the conflict? Every story must have a conflict to be of interest. Is it between characters, the character and the environment, or the character's development within himself?

- Make the ending resolve the conflict.

The following ideas for writing fictional stories work well as an introduction to this type of writing because they are very motivational.

Primary

- The Santa Who Lost His Way
- The Night Rudolph's Nose Wouldn't Light
- The Night Santa Got Stuck in My Chimney
- The Night Santa Found a Hole in His Bag
- The Very Strange Winter
- When I Woke Up I Was the Smartest Child in the World
- A Day in the Life of a Snowflake
- The Day I Grew Wings
- A Blizzard

Upper Grades

- Have the students write a story where someone makes a wrong decision and gets deeper and deeper into the problem they have created. They then have to get themselves out of trouble. This may be the time to teach quotation marks and dialogue if this is new or if students need a review.

- A wonderful writing idea comes from the Chris Van Allsburg book, *The Mysteries of Harris Burdick*. This book is available in the picture book or regular section of most school libraries. In the introduction, which is crucial to the book, we find that a publisher has a number of drawings with captions that were dropped off by a man named Harris Burdick. Mr. Burdick, who was supposed to return the next day to bring the rest of the material, never returned to the publisher's office. The publisher still has all of Mr. Burdick's drawings and captions years later. The readers are invited to tell the story that goes with each picture and caption. This is an opportunity for each student to choose an illustration and write a story to go with it. Most of the students really enjoy this activity.

- *Over Thanksgiving break I . . .*
- *My plans for winter break are . . .*
- *If I were not in school today*
- *My favorite book is . . . because . . .*
- *Right now my biggest problem is . . .*
- *The best way to make a friend*
- *My favorite season of the year is . . . because . . .*
- *A character from fiction I might like to meet is . . . because . . .*

Poems to Memorize

2nd grade: "The Wrong Start," by Marchette Chute, is an *Alexander and the . . . Bad Day* style poem, *Random House Book of Poetry.*

3rd grade: "No One Else," by Elaine Laron, from *Free to Be You and Me,* Bantam Books, is a poem about the uniqueness of each of us.

4th grade: "Stopping by Woods," by Robert Frost, *Random House Book of Poetry.* This poem is appropriate for all three of these grades. It describes a man stopping in the woods on a cold evening and his horse's urgings to hurry home. It is a perfect poem for this time of year.

5th grade: same as 4th grade.

6th grade: same as 4th grade.

Note your special poems for memorization

_____

_____

_____

_____

Poems to Write

Haiku

During the busy month of December, it is fun to write short, winter poems. A good style is the Japanese haiku poem. This is a seventeen-syllable poem with three lines — line one has five syllables, line two has seven syllables, and line three has five syllables. All lines describe one subject. This is a wonderful poem with which to do a winter art project. On the left below are two samples.

Snow

Snow
Snow gently falling
Landing softly on my face
Melting quickly — gone

Trees

Trees
Bare of all their leaves
Winter fiercely beating them
Spring brings life again

aud - hear or listen

audible: can be heard

audience: a group of listeners

auditorium: a building used for audience assembly

audio: relating to sound by electric currents

audiometer: an instrument by which hearing can be measured

inaudible: cannot be heard

auditory: relating to hearing

audiovisual: sound accompanying pictures

audition: a hearing

auditor: one who listens

super - over, beyond, greater in quantity

superman: a man with extraordinary powers

superiority: excellence

supervise: to oversee

superlative: in the highest degree

supreme: superior; of the highest quality

supremacy: state of being supreme

Primary

- January is the first month of the year. It is named for Janus, a Roman god. This month and February were added to the ten-month Roman calendar about 700 B.C.
- The January flower is the carnation, and the birthstone is the garnet.
- In this month or February, Chinese New Year occurs. It takes place with the first new moon after the sun enters Aquarius. Each new year is named for one of twelve animals. Gifts of fruit and red envelopes of money are given to children at this time.

1. This is New Year's Day. Many people celebrate the beginning of a new year by making resolutions.

1. The first U.S. Tournament of Roses Parade took place in Pasadena, California in 1886.

1. This is the birthday of Betsy Ross. It is said that she made the first American flag.

2. Georgia became the fourth U.S. state in 1788. Georgia is the largest state east of the Mississippi River.

3. On this day in 1938 the March of Dimes campaign was organized to collect money to fight polio.

3. Alaska became the forty-ninth state in 1959. Alaska is more than twice as big as Texas, our second largest state.

4. This is the birth date of Jacob Grimm. He and his brother Wilhelm are famous for their collections of German fairy tales. He was born in Germany in 1785.

4. Louis Braille was born on this date in 1809. He was a blind man from France who developed an alphabet that blind people could read.

5. This is the birth date of George Washington Carver. Although he was born a slave, he became one of America's leading scientists. He found more than 300 products that could be made from the peanut.

5. Nellie Taylor Ross was the first woman to be sworn in as a governor of a state. She took office in Wyoming in 1925.

6. New Mexico became the forty-seventh U.S. state in 1912. Carlsbad Caverns National Park, the home of huge caves filled with bats, is in New Mexico.

7. The first American presidential election was held on this day in 1789.

7. This is the birthday of Millard Fillmore, who was the thirteenth U.S. president. He was born in 1800.

8. This is the birthday of American singer Elvis Presley. He was born in 1935.

9. Connecticut became the fifth U.S. state in 1788. Connecticut is famous for its lovely old towns.

9. Richard Nixon was born on this date in 1913. He was the thirty-seventh president.

10. The League of Nations was founded in 1920 after World War I. Its purpose was to join nations together to prevent future wars.

12. John Hancock was born on this day in 1737. He was a famous American patriot who is especially well-known for his signature on the Declaration of Independence.

12. Charles Perrault was born on this day in 1628. He was the French author of "Cinderella" and "Sleeping Beauty."

13. This is Stephen Foster Memorial Day. Foster was the composer of many songs. He wrote "Oh! Susanna" and "My Old Kentucky Home."

15. Martin Luther King, Jr. was born on January 15, 1929. He was an American civil rights leader who is famous for his nonviolent actions in seeking equal rights for all Americans. He won the Nobel Peace Prize.

17. Benjamin Franklin was an American inventor, statesman, and author of <u>Poor Richard's Almanac</u>. He was born on this day in 1706.

18. A. A. Milne was born on this day in 1882. He was the English author of <u>Winnie the Pooh</u>.

18. On this day in 1778 Captain James Cook discovered the Hawaiian Islands. He named them the Sandwich Islands after Lord Sandwich.

20. This is Inauguration Day. On this day every four years the president of the United States takes office.

23. On this day in 1849 Elizabeth Blackwell became the first American woman to become a medical doctor.

24. On this day in 1848 James Marshall discovered gold while working at Sutter's Mill in California.

24. In 1908 Robert Baden-Powell organized the first Boy Scout troop in England.

25. The first Winter Olympics took place on this day in 1924 in Chamonix, France.

26. This is Australia Day. The country was first settled by colonists on this date in 1788.

26. Michigan became the twenty-sixth state in 1837. Michigan is the only state divided into two parts.

27. This is the birthday of Lewis Carroll. He was born in 1832. Carroll wrote <u>Alice's Adventures in Wonderland</u> for the daughter of a friend.

29. This is the birth date of William McKinley. He was the twenty-fifth president of the United States.

29. Kansas became the thirty-fourth state on this date in 1861. Kansas grows so much wheat it is called the "bread-basket of America."

29. Children's author, Bill Peet, was born on this day. He wrote <u>Big Bad Bruce</u>.

30. Franklin D. Roosevelt was the thirty-second president of the Untied States. He was born on this day in 1882.

31. In 1959 the first U.S. satellite was launched. It was called <u>Explorer I</u>.

31. Jackie Robinson was born on this day in 1919. Robinson was the first black individual to enter the major leagues. He is a member of the Baseball Hall of Fame.

Upper Grades

- January is the first month of the year. It is named for Janus, a Roman god. He is always shown with two faces, looking into the past and the future. This month and February were added to the ten-month Roman calendar about 700 B.C.
- The January flower is the carnation, and the birthstone is the garnet.
- In this month or February, Chinese New Year occurs. It takes place with the first new moon after the sun enters Aquarius. Each new year is named for one of twelve animals. Gifts of fruit and red envelopes of money are given to children at this time.

1. This is the birthday of Betsy Ross, who was born on this day in 1752. It is said that she made the first United States flag in her shop in Philadelphia, Pennsylvania.

1. Famous patriot Paul Revere was born on this day in 1735. He is known for taking part in the Boston Tea Party and riding to warn the patriots that the British troops were coming on April 18, 1775.

1. On this day in 1863 Abraham Lincoln issued the Emancipation Proclamation. This famous document freed the slaves.

2. Georgia became the fourth U.S. state in 1788. Georgia is the largest state east of the Mississippi River.

3. This is the birthday of famous abolitionist and women's rights leader Lucretia Mott.

3. Today is the birthday of J. R. R. Tolkien, English author of <u>The Hobbit</u> and other books. He was born in 1892.

3. On this day in 1938 the March of Dimes campaign was organized to collect money to fight polio.

3. Alaska became the forty-ninth state in 1959. Alaska is more than twice as big as Texas, our second largest state.

4. This is the birth date of Jacob Grimm. He and his brother Wilhelm are famous for their collections of German fairy tales. Jacob Grimm was born in Germany in 1785.

4. Louis Braille, the designer of the Braille alphabet, was born on this date in 1809. He was a blind Frenchman who developed an alphabet that blind people could read.

4. Utah became the forty-fifth state on this day in 1896. Utah contains the Great Salt Lake, which is four times saltier than any ocean.

5. On this day in 1925 the first woman to be sworn in as a governor of a state, Mrs. Nellie Taylor Ross, took office in Wyoming.

5. This is the birthday of George Washington Carver. Although Carver was born a slave, he became one of America's leading scientists. He worked to help the South by developing products that could be made from plants grown there. He was known as "the plant doctor."

6. Carl Sandburg, famous American poet, was born on this day in 1878. Sandburg won the Pulitzer Prize for his work.

6. New Mexico became the forty-seventh state in 1912. Carlsbad Caverns National Park, home of huge caves of bats, is in New Mexico.

7. The first American presidential election was held on this day in 1789.

7. The first transatlantic commercial telephone service began between New York and London in 1927.

7. Millard Fillmore, the thirteenth U.S. president, was born on this day in 1800. He became president when Zachary Taylor died on July 9, 1850.

7. Galileo discovered the moons of Jupiter on January 7, 1610.

7. Boston, Massachusetts cooking instructor Fannie Farmer first published her now-famous cookbook in 1896. She was the first to standardize measurements in cookbooks, instead of using "a bit," "a touch," "a scoop," and "some."

8. This is the birthday of American singer Elvis Presley. He was born in 1935.

9. Connecticut became the fifth U.S. state in 1788. Connecticut is famous for its lovely old towns.

9. Richard Milhous Nixon, thirty-seventh president, was born on this date in 1913. He resigned from office when he knew he would be impeached for lying and taking part in a coverup.

10. The League of Nations was founded in 1920, following World War I. Its purpose was to join nations together to prevent future wars.

10. On this date in 1776 Thomas Paine published his famous pamphlet, Common Sense. This pamphlet stated the reasons for separation of the Colonies from England.

11. Statesman and the first Secretary of State Alexander Hamilton was born on this day in 1755.

12. John Hancock, American patriot, was born on this day in 1737. Today we know him for his famous signature on the Declaration of Independence.

12. Charles Perrault was born on this day in 1628. He was the French author of "Cinderella" and "Sleeping Beauty."

13. In 1733 James Oglethorpe, along with 130 other colonists, established a settlement in what is now the state of Georgia.

13. This is Stephen Foster Memorial Day. Foster was the composer of many songs. He wrote "Oh! Susanna" and "My Old Kentucky Home," as well as many more American classics.

14. This is the birthday of Albert Schweitzer. He was a physician, musician, philosopher, and missionary. He was born on this day in 1875. He is especially famous for his work in Africa, where he and others built a hospital and established a leper colony. He was awarded the Nobel Peace Prize.

14. This is the birthday of Benedict Arnold, Revolutionary War traitor. He was an American general who worked for the enemy for sixteen months.

15. Martin Luther King, Jr. was born on January 15, 1929. He was an American civil rights leader who is famous for his nonviolent actions in seeking equal rights for all Americans. He won the Nobel Peace Prize.

17. Benjamin Franklin was born in Boston, Massachusetts on this date in 1706. He was an American inventor, statesman, and author of Poor Richard's Almanac. He helped develop the Declaration of Independence and proved that lightning was electricity.

18. This is the birth date of A. A. Milne, author of Winnie the Pooh. He wrote his books about his son's stuffed animals. Milne was born in 1882 and lived until 1956.

18. On this day in 1778 Captain James Cook discovered the Hawaiian Islands, naming them the Sandwich Islands after Lord Sandwich.

19. American author Edgar Allan Poe was born in 1809. One of his most famous works was "The Raven."

19. This is the birthday of Robert E. Lee. He was a famous Confederate general during the Civil War.

19. In 1840 Captain Charles Wilkes discovered the coast of Antarctica.

20. This is Inauguration Day. On this day every four years the president of the United States takes office.

21. Ethan Allen, American patriot and leader of the Green Mountain Boys during the American Revolutionary War, was born on this day in 1738.

23. On this day in 1849 Elizabeth Blackwell became the first American woman to become a medical doctor.

24. On this day in 1848 James Marshall discovered gold at Sutter's Mill in what is now California. This discovery led to thousands settling in the area and eventually resulted in statehood.

24. The first public meeting of the English Boy Scouts took place on this day in 1908.

25. Transcontinental telephone service was established in the United States when Alexander Bell in New York City talked to his assistant in San Francisco on this day in 1915.

25. The first Winter Olympics took place on this day in 1924 in Chamonix, France.

26. This is Australia Day. The country was first settled by colonists on this date in 1788.

26. Michigan became the twenty-sixth state in 1837. Michigan is the only state divided into two parts.

27. The National Geographic Society was started in 1888 in Washington D.C.

27. This is the birthday of Lewis Carroll. He was born in 1832. Carroll wrote Alice's Adventures in Wonderland for the daughter of a friend.

27. The Canadian Great Western Railway started operating on this day in 1854.

27. Wolfgang Amadeus Mozart, Austrian composer, was born on this day in 1736. He was a musical prodigy who played several instruments and composed music by the age of six.

28. On this day in 1986 the Challenger 2 spacecraft exploded just after takeoff. Seven astronauts perished in this tragic accident.

28. The U.S. Coast Guard was established in 1915.

29. This is the birth date of William McKinley, the twenty-fifth president of the United States. He was born on this day in 1843. During his term, Hawaii became an American territory. McKinley was shot and killed by an anarchist in 1901.

29. Kansas became the thirty-fourth state on this date in 1861. Kansas grows so much wheat it is called the "bread-basket of America."

30. The first five players elected to the Baseball Hall of Fame in 1936 were Walter Johnson, Christy Mathewson, Honus Wagner, Babe Ruth, and Ty Cobb.

30. Congress authorized the purchase of Thomas Jefferson's library as the nucleus of the Library of Congress in 1815.

30. Our thirty-second president, Franklin D. Roosevelt, was born on this date in 1882. He was elected four times. Roosevelt led the United States through the Depression and World War II.

30. This is the birthday of children's author Lloyd Alexander, who wrote The Book of Three.

31. Jackie Robinson was born on this day in 1919. Robinson was the first black individual to enter the major leagues. He is a member of the Baseball Hall of Fame.

31. In 1959 the first U.S. satellite, Explorer I, was launched.

31. Austrian composer of symphonies Franz Schubert was born on this day in 1797.

Point of View

A wonderful way to get students to write is to provide them with an already-structured story. In this writing lesson, the students take the point of view of someone in the story or article. For instance, in the book, *The True Story of the Three Little Pigs,* by Jon Scieszka, the wolf tells the story from his point of view. Be sure to discuss what a point of view is, stressing how we each see things a little differently.

In the sample newspaper article, a fox has been stealing shoes left outside of homes for a long period of time. Wondering who has been stealing everyone's shoes, a young boy sets up an alarm to catch the thief. He discovers that a fox has stolen three hundred shoes and six baseball mitts and taken them to a gully.

For this lesson, begin by having students listen carefully to the article. After it has been read to them, ask them to state facts that they have learned. Put these facts on the board as they provide them. Then read the article once more. Ask if there are any corrections or additions to the list.

After these corrections are made, ask the students who they think could tell the story. They will probably say that the newspaper reporter, the boy, the step-father, a neighbor, or the fox could tell the story. Some may even suggest the shoe. At this time, with all the facts on the board, have each student choose a point of view from which to tell the story and begin to write what happened from that individual's point of view. Remind them to include as many descriptive details as possible.

This is a fun and successful lesson. Because they don't have to worry about a story framework, they are free to concentrate on style.

Articles for this assignment are available in any newspaper. Look for ones that have a difficult situation that is solved and also a little bit of humor. The story, too, must be long enough to write about in some depth.

The Sneaky Fox Family

In Santa Barbara, California recently, a family of red foxes stole hundreds of shoes left outside homes.

Residents in a hilly area of Santa Barbara had been upset for months about the loss of shoes left outside their homes. They thought that hundreds of their shoes had been stolen, including $120 basketball shoes and $80 topsiders.

Last week a twelve-year-old boy, Tim Jones, decided to set a trap for the thief. He hooked up an electric horn and a pressure switch. That evening he went to bed. About midnight the horn went off and he went to investigate.

After he awakened his step-father, the two of them searched the neighborhood. They were able to spot a young red fox who was dragging one of Tim's tennis shoes. Tim and his father followed the fox to a canyon filled with brush. When they arrived, they spotted three hundred shoes and six baseball mitts.

When the word got out that the fox family was the guilty party, everyone in the neighborhood was less angry and slightly amused as they visited Tim's house to retrieve their shoes.

- *Over winter break, I . . . (Tell a little about your vacation.)*
- *My New Year's resolutions*
- *If I could shrink to microscopic size*
- *An animal I would like to be for a day is . . . because . . .*
- *A good cure for sadness is . . .*
- *Write a description of one member of your family. Tell what they are like inside and outside.*
- *If I had a suitcase as large as the top of my desk and about five inches deep and were going on a submarine for a month and had to plan carefully, these are the things that I would put in my suitcase and these are the reasons I would take these items.*
- *If I were invisible for one day, I would . . .*
- *If someone were to give me three books as a gift, I would choose . . . because . . .*
- *My favorite restaurant is . . . because . . .*

Poems to Memorize

2nd grade: "This Book Belongs to Me," by Arnold Lobel, *Once Upon a Time.* G. P. Putnam's Sons Sons. All children love to own books. This poem is about that special fondness for owning a book.

3rd grade: "Who Has Seen the Wind," by Christina Rossetti, from *Sing a Song of Popcorn*, Scholastic. As the wind begins to blow at this time of the year, children will enjoy this famous poem.

4th grade: "I Met a Dragon," by Jack Prelutsky, from *Good Books, Good Times!,* selected by Lee Bennett Hopkins, Harper & Row. This is about all the characters readers meet in the books they read.

5th grade: same as 4th grade.

6th grade: "Snowflakes," by Frank Asch, from *Sing a Song of Popcorn,* Scholastic.

Note your special poems for memorization

_____

_____

_____

_____

Poems to Write

Copy Change

Copy change is an effective way to get students to begin to write poetry. With this technique, students begin with a basic framework, yet add their own ideas. From this simple, structured beginning they are more comfortable with their own writing and ready to express themselves with their own form, style, and ideas.

Suggested Poems

There are many poems that work beautifully with the concept of copy change. Judith Viorst's poem, "If I Were in Charge of the World," from the book *If I Were in Charge of the World and Other Worries,* Athenaeum Macmillan Publishing Company, is a delightful poem for this method. Another favorite is

"Knoxville, Tennessee" by Nikki Giovanni, from the book *Knoxville, Tennessee*, Scholastic. In it she describes her home town in the summer. The words can easily be changed to describe your home town, favorite summer foods, and places to go. Another effective poem to use is "The Tiniest Sound," by Mel Evans from the book *The Tiniest Sound*, Doubleday. Once you have used this method, you'll find many poems that work well for copy changing.

An Example

The following poem, "The Softest Sound," is a result of changing the copy in "The Tiniest Sound." You can use the poem "The Tiniest Sound" to copy change, or you can begin with the poem "The Softest Sound" that follows.

Read one of the poems with students. Then have them write their own poems, keeping the format of three stanzas and retaining the first two lines of each stanza ("The softest sound might be," "Perhaps the softest sound I can imagine," and "As I lie dreaming the softest sound I hear"). To complete the poems, they should think of three soft sounds and add a description of one sound to each of the three stanzas. This copy change lesson usually works best if it is presented over a period of three days.

The Softest Sound

The softest sound
might be
the sun coming up.
Over the hills it silently
rises
too slowly
for anyone to see movement,
yet steadily rising until
it reaches high in the sky
only to retreat and appear
again
each day.

Perhaps the softest sound
I can imagine
is a butterfly
gently landing
on a delicate lilac blossom,
dropping ever so quietly
until it stops,
barely touching
the perfect flower.

As I lie dreaming
the softest sound I hear
is the gentle breeze
touching my cheeks,
rocking me to sleep,
soft as a baby's
tiny
fingers.

fact and **fac** - to make

factor: one of the elements contributing to a situation

factory: the place where workers are employed in making goods

facilitate: to make easy to do

manufacturer: the owner of a factory

dissatisfaction: the state of being made unhappy

facsimile: a copy that is exact in every detail

scrib and **scrip** - to write

scribble: meaningless marks on paper

description: a representation in words of something seen

inscription: words engraved on a stone or monument

subscription: sign one's name for acceptance

prescription: written directions from a doctor for preparation of medicine

script: written characters; also short for manuscript

transcript: a copy of something in writing

scribe: a public writer acting as clerk

photo - having to do with light

photogenic: capable of being photographed well

photograph: a picture made by the reaction of light on a special plate

photon: a unit of light intensity

photometer: an instrument for measuring the intensity of light.

Primary

- February is the second month of the year and the shortest month. According to legend, Romulus did not include it when he made the first Roman calendar, which had only ten months. Numa Pompilus, who followed Romulus, added two months, making February the last month of the year. Julius Caesar moved the beginning of the year from March to January, making February the second month.
- February usually has twenty-eight days. February had thirty days until the time of Julius Caesar. Caesar took one day from this month to add to the month named after him, July. Emperor Augustus took another day off to add to August, the month named after him.
- See January for Chinese New Year.
- The primrose and the violet are the special flowers for February. The amethyst is the birthstone.

1. Today is the birthday of black author and poet Langston Hughes. He was born in 1902.

1. On this day in 1884 the first volume of the Oxford English Dictionary, A-Ant, was published.

2. This is the birthday of children's author Judith Viorst. She wrote Alexander and the Terrible, Horrible, No Good, Very Bad Day.

2. This is Groundhog Day.

3. American artist Norman Rockwell was born on this day in 1894.

4. Charles A. Lindbergh was the first aviator to make a solo transatlantic flight. He was born on this day in 1902.

4. The first Winter Olympics to be held in the United States took place in Lake Placid, New York in 1934.

4. Russell Hoban wrote the Frances series. He was born on this day.

6. Hank Aaron was baseball's "Home Run King." He was born on this day in 1932.

6. Massachusetts was the sixth state to join the Union. Massachusetts is famous for many things, including having the first Thanksgiving and the first battles of the Revolutionary War.

6. This is the birthday of Babe Ruth, whose real name was George Herman Ruth. He was a baseball great and member of the Baseball Hall of Fame.

6. This is the birthday of Ronald Reagan. He was the fortieth president of the United States. He was born in 1911.

7. This is the birthday of Laura Ingalls Wilder, author of the Little House books. She was born on this day in 1867.

8. Jules Verne, was a famous author of science fiction stories. He was born on this day in 1828. He wrote Twenty Thousand Leagues Under the Sea.

8. In 1910 the Boy Scouts of America was founded by William Boyce.

9. The United States Weather Service was established in 1870.

9. This is the birthday of William Henry Harrison. He was the ninth president of the United States. He was born in 1773 and died one month after taking office.

10. This is the birthday of Mark Spitz, who was born in 1950. Spitz set a world record at the 1972 Olympic Games in Munich by winning seven gold medals.

11. The first hospital in America was opened in Philadelphia, Pennsylvania in 1751.

11. Thomas Alva Edison was an American inventor. He was born on this day in 1847. He invented more than 1,000 new products.

12. This is the birthday of children's author Judy Blume.

12. Abraham Lincoln, our sixteenth president, was born on this day in 1809. He was elected president in 1860 and 1864. Many people called him "Honest Abe."

13. The first public school opened on this day in 1635. It was the Boston Latin School.

13. The first magazine in the United States was published on this day in 1741. It was named The American Magazine.

14. Today is St. Valentine's Day. People have been giving valentines for hundreds of years.

14. Arizona became the forty-eighth state in 1912. Arizona has the world's largest canyon, the Grand Canyon.

14. Oregon became the thirty-third state in 1859. Crater Lake is in Oregon. It is the deepest lake in the United States at 1,932 feet deep.

15. Susan B. Anthony was born on this day in 1820. She worked for women's right to vote, women's property rights, and abolition of slavery.

16. The first television news program was broadcast on this day in 1948.

17. The P.T.A., Parent Teacher Association, was established on this day in 1897.

18. The planet Pluto was seen for the first time in 1930 by astronomer Clyde Tombaugh.

19. Nicholas Copernicus was born on this day in 1473. He found that the sun is the center of the solar system.

19. Thomas Edison was issued a patent for his invention, the phonograph, in 1877.

20. In 1962 U.S. astronaut John Glenn orbited the earth three times in a space capsule.

20. In 1965 the Ranger 8 spacecraft landed on the moon and sent back to Earth pictures of the lunar surface.

20. The Metropolitan Museum of Art opened on this date in New York City in 1872. It is the largest art museum in the United States.

21. The first telephone directory was issued in 1878 by the New Haven, Connecticut Telephone Company.

22. February 22, 1732, is the birth date of George Washington, our first president.

22. The United States bought the Florida territory from Spain in 1819.

25. The Ranger, the first United States aircraft carrier, was launched on this day in 1934.

25. In 1928 a New York paper reported on the latest national craze, dance marathons.

26. William Cody was born on this day in 1846. He was known as Buffalo Bill. He was an American frontiersman and scout.

26. Grand Canyon National Park was established in 1919.

29. Every four years leap year is celebrated. Because our year is 365 days and six hours long, we add an extra day every four years.

Upper Grades

- February is the second month of the year and the shortest month. According to legend, Romulus did not include it when he made the first Roman calendar, which had only ten months. Numa Pompilus, who followed Romulus, added two months, making February the last month of the year. Julius Caesar moved the beginning of the year from March to January, making February the second month.

- **February usually has twenty-eight days.** February had thirty days until the time of Julius Caesar. Caesar took one day from this month to add to the month named after him, July. Emperor Augustus took another day off to add to August, the month named after him.

- February is Black History Month.

- See January for Chinese New Year.

- The primrose and the violet are the special flowers for February. The amethyst is the birthstone.

1. The Supreme Court of the United States met for the first time in 1790.

1. Today is the birthday of black author and poet Langston Hughes. He was born in 1902. Included in his work is <u>The Dream Keeper and Other Poems</u>.

1. On this day in 1884 the first volume of the <u>Oxford English Dictionary, A-Ant</u>, was published.

2. This is the birthday of children's author Judith Viorst. Students enjoy her books and poems.

2. Today is Groundhog Day. The most famous groundhog is Punxsutawney Phil. He lives near the small Pennsylvania town of Punxsutawney. It is said that if he sees his shadow when he comes out of his hole on February 2, there will be six more weeks of bad weather.

3. Elizabeth Blackwell was born on this day in 1821. She was the first female doctor in the United States. She applied to twenty-nine medical schools before being accepted.

3. American artist Norman Rockwell was born on this day in 1894.

4. The first Winter Olympics held in the United States was held in Lake Placid, New York in 1932.

4. Charles A. Lindbergh was born on this day in 1902. Lindbergh made the first nonstop solo flight across the Atlantic Ocean. He flew from New York to Paris.

4. The Confederate States of America were formed by a temporary committee meeting in Montgomery, Alabama in 1861.

4. The Twenty-fourth Amendment to the U.S. Constitution was added in 1964. It banned the poll tax.

5. Hank Aaron, baseball's "Home Run King," was born on this day in 1934.

6. Massachusetts was the sixth state to ratify the Constitution, making it our sixth state. This took place in 1788. Massachusetts is famous for many firsts, including the first Thanksgiving and the first battles of the Revolutionary War.

6. Aaron Burr, American political leader, was born on this day in 1756.

6. This is the birthday of Babe Ruth, whose real name was George Herman Ruth. He was a baseball great and member of the Baseball Hall of Fame.

6. This is the birthday of Ronald Reagan, fortieth president of the United States. He was born on this day in 1911.

7. This is the birthday of Laura Ingalls Wilder, author of the Little House books. She was born on this day in 1867.

7. English author Charles Dickens was born on this day in 1812. He wrote books like Oliver Twist and A Christmas Carol.

7. Frederick Douglass, American abolitionist, was born on this day in 1817.

8. In 1910 the Boy Scouts of America was founded by William Boyce.

8. Famous novelist Jules Verne was born on this day in 1823. One of his most well-known works is Twenty Thousand Leagues Under the Sea.

9. The United States Weather Service was established in 1870.

9. This is the birthday of William Henry Harrison, the ninth president of the United States. He was born in 1773. After working hard on his campaign he caught a cold that turned into pneumonia. Harrison died one month after his inauguration.

9. Jefferson Davis was elected president of the Confederacy on this day in 1861.

10. This is the birthday of Mark Spitz, who was born in 1950. Spitz set a world record at the 1972 Olympic Games in Munich, Germany by winning seven gold medals.

11. Nelson Mandela was released from a South African prison in 1990. He had been jailed for twenty-seven years because of his role in fighting against apartheid in his country.

11. Thomas Alva Edison, American inventor, was born on this day in 1847. He invented more than 1,000 new products. While searching for the right material to burn in a light bulb, he tried 6,000 different things before he found the one he wanted. He invented the phonograph and motion pictures.

11. The first hospital in America was opened in Philadelphia, Pennsylvania, on this date in 1751.

12. The sixteenth president, Abraham Lincoln, was born on this day in 1809. He was elected president in 1860 and 1864. He was president during the Civil War. He was assassinated before his second term ended.

12. This is the birthday of children's author Judy Blume.

13. The first public school opened on this day in 1635. It was the Boston Latin School.

13. The first magazine in the United States, American Magazine, was published on this day in 1741. It was followed three days later by Benjamin Franklin's General Magazine.

14. Today is St. Valentine's Day. It may have been named after a Christian named Valentine who was imprisoned by the Romans because he would not give up his Christian faith. The daughter of his jailer became his friend and Valentine wrote her a note before he was executed and signed it "Your Valentine." He was later made a saint and Valentine's Day is sometimes called St. Valentine's Day.

14. Oregon became the thirty-third state in 1859. Oregon contains Crater Lake, the deepest lake in the United States. It is 1,932 feet deep.

14. Arizona became the forty-eighth state in 1912. Arizona has the world's largest canyon, the Grand Canyon.

15. Galileo Galilei, Italian astronomer and physicist, was born on this day in 1564.

15. Susan B. Anthony was born in 1820. She worked for women's right to vote, women's property rights, and the abolition of slavery.

16. The first television news program was broadcast on this day in 1948.

17. The P.T.A., Parent Teacher Association, was established on this day in 1897.

18. The planet Pluto was seen for the first time in 1930 by astronomer Clyde Tombaugh. He saw it in photographs he took at the Lowell Observatory in Flagstaff, Arizona.

19. Nicholas Copernicus was born on this day in 1473. He found that the sun is the center of the solar system

19. Thomas Edison patented the phonograph on this day in 1878.

20. The United States mail service was established in 1792.

20. On this date in 1962 United States astronaut John Glenn orbited the earth three times in a space capsule.

20. In 1965 the Ranger 8 spacecraft landed on the moon and sent back to Earth pictures of the lunar surface.

20. The Metropolitan Museum of Art opened on this day in 1872 in New York City. It is the largest art museum in the United States.

21. The first telephone directory was issued in 1878 by the New Haven, Connecticut Telephone Company.

22. February 22, 1732, is the birth date of George Washington, our first president. He also served as commander of the American army throughout the Revolutionary War.

23. George Frideric Handel was born on this day in 1685. He was a German-English composer of operas and orchestra music. He is considered one of the greatest musicians of all time.

24. Winslow Homer, American marine artist, was born on this day in 1836.

24. In 1803 Chief Justice John Marshall presided over one of the most important cases ever decided by the Supreme Court. The Supreme Court ruled that it has the power to invalidate any law of Congress that is, in its opinion, unconstitutional.

25. Pierre Auguste Renoir was born on this day in 1841. He was a French impressionist painter.

25. The Ranger, the first United States aircraft carrier, was launched on this day in 1934.

25. The Sixteenth Amendment to the United States Constitution became law on this day in 1913. This gave Congress the power to collect taxes based on a person's income.

25. In 1928 a New York paper reported on the latest national craze, dance marathons.

25. This is the birthday of author of books for young people, Cynthia Voigt.

26. William Cody, also known as Buffalo Bill, was born on this day in 1846. He was an American frontiersman and scout.

26. Grand Canyon National Park was established in Arizona in 1919.

27. American poet Henry Wadsworth Longfellow was born on this day in 1807. One of his most popular poems is "Paul Revere's Ride."

27. This is the birthday of Ralph Nader, American consumer advocate, who was born in 1934.

29. Every four years leap year is celebrated. Because our year is 365 days and six hours long, we add an extra day every four years.

Fairy Tales

Fairy tales are a wonderful writing genre to work with at any grade level. Because many parents don't have the time to read traditional fairy tales to their children, you may choose to share some of these stories with your class. Even upper grade students enjoy most fairy tales and especially like hearing tales from around the world. See if you can find various versions of "Cinderella" from different countries, for example.

Incorporating Fairy Tales

As you read fairy tales, here are some writing activities that will allow you to develop writing skills as an extension of your literature unit.

- Make a fairy tale into a news article that includes information about who, what, when, where, and why.
- Write a letter to one of the characters giving him or her gentle advice.
- Write a letter to a character, have her or him write back, and then you write back again.
- Write a new ending to a fairy tale.

- Write a two-word-per-line poem about your fairy tale. See the example in February Poems to Write.
- Write an acrostic poem about a character in your fairy tale. See the example in February Poems to Write.
- Write a limerick about your fairy tale. See the example in February Poems to Write.
- Have any of the characters committed a crime? Write a short play involving a judge and jury.
- Write a recipe for a good fairy tale. Be sure to list ingredients and steps.
- Choose a fairy tale and tell it from a different point of view.
- Make a travel brochure for the land in which the fairy tale occurred.
- Design and write a postcard from the fairy tale's setting. Decide who is writing it, who he or she is sending it to, and then write the message.
- Combine characters or elements from two fairy tales and make a new interesting story.

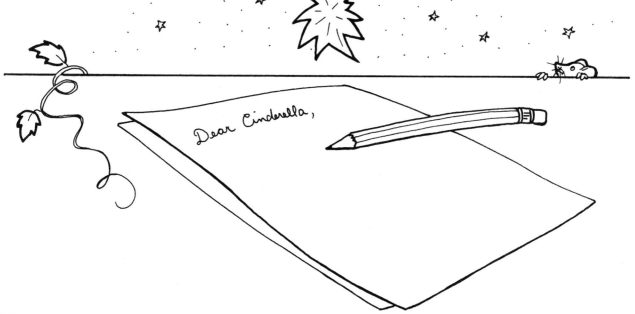

- *My favorite family dinner is . . . because . . .*
- *Three rules a friend should follow are . . .*
- *The best place to be alone is . . . because . . .*
- *I don't like to be disturbed when . . .*
- *I will never forget the time . . .*
- *I would like to invent a machine that would . . .*
- *If I could live in another time period it would be . . . because . . .*
- *The five things that make me the happiest are . . .*
- *An old toy I enjoyed*
- *I have difficulty trying to deal with . . .*

Poems to Memorize

2nd grade: "Deaf Donald," by Shel Silverstein, from *A Light in the Attic,* Harper & Row, is a sweet poem about communication that has accompanying sign language.

3rd grade: same as 2nd grade.

4th grade: "The Wind," by James Reeves, *The Random House Book of Poetry,* Random House, is about the ability of the wind to be powerful enough to do damage yet gentle enough to carry the scent of a flower.

5th grade: "Whatif," by Shel Silverstein, from *A Light in the Attic,* Harper & Row, is a poem about all the worries children have.

6th grade: same as 5th grade.

Note your special poems for memorization

_____

_____

_____

_____

Poems to Write

Fairy Tale Poetry

While you are studying and writing fairy tales during this month, it is a good opportunity to extend your unit and write poetry that relates to fairy tales or fairy tale characters. Here are three ideas to tie poetry in with a fairy tale unit.

■ ■ ■ ■ ■ ■ ■ ■ ■ ■ ■

Two-Word Fairy Tale Poems

The instructions for this poem are given on page 24. The following example is a poem about Little Red Riding Hood.

LITTLE RED RIDING HOOD

Hooded girl

Visits grandmother.

Bad wolf

Arrived previously.

Ate grandmother.

Tricks girl.

Brave woodsman's

Timely arrival

Saves all.

Fairy Tale Limerick

A limerick is a difficult style of poem used best by fifth and sixth graders. It is a five-line poem with the format a, a, b, b, a. This means that the first two lines rhyme with each other, the third and fourth lines rhyme with each other, and the last line rhymes with the first two lines. There is also a certain rhythm to a limerick that students can easily hear. It is a short story within a very short poem. The first four lines introduce the main character and the conflict. The last line concludes and solves the conflict either in a positive or negative manner.

There are many books on limericks available in school libraries, including Arnold Lobel's *Pigericks*, to use as examples. The following is an example of a limerick written about a fairy tale character, Cinderella. After sharing the poem with students, have them choose a fairy tale character and write their own limericks.

Cinderella

There once was a pretty young dame
Whose sisters gave her a cindery name.
One night she went to the dance,
Put the prince in a trance.
And her life was never the same.

Fairy Tale Acrostics

In an acrostic poem, a word is spelled going down the page in larger or darker letters. The word that is chosen may be a character, a place, or a characteristic. Words are then chosen that start with each of the letters to describe the word. In the following examples, words describe the words "wolf" and "witch."

Witty	*Witty*
Ornery	*Irresponsible*
Listener	*Tricky*
Fast	*Clever*
	Hovering

Alliteration

Alliteration is not a poem itself, but a technique to enhance appreciation of poetry and vocabulary development. The students always enjoy finding clever words with the same letter or sound, and they quickly learn that they can add alliterative phrases to give a musical quality to nearly any poem.

Alliteration is the same letter or sound in words succeeding each other at close intervals. There are many fun ideas to use for teaching the concept of alliteration to students. To start with, have the students orally fill in the blanks with words that begin with the same letters as most of the other words in the sentence. This will help them understand the basic concept of alliteration.

1. Linda lived in a lodge and liked_____for lunch.

2. Fred found a frog and fed it _____.

3. We went to the well to get_____for_____ .

4. Paul put the perfect plant on the ____ in the_____.

Writing Alliterative Sentences

Here is a very effective way of combining a lesson on parts of speech with alliteration:

1. On the board write:

____ ____ ____ ____ ____ ____
  adj   adj   noun adv verb noun

2. Ask someone in class to give you a noun that begins with a letter of your choice. (Of course, some letters are easier to work with than others, so choose an easy letter for demonstration purposes.)

3. Write that word on the line above "noun" (example: *salmon*).

4. Ask for one or two adjectives that begin with the same letter and fill in those blanks.
several silly salmon
 adj.   adj.   noun

5. Ask for a verb and then an adverb.

6. Complete with "where."

several silly salmon swiftly swam south
 adj.   adj.   noun   adv.   verb. noun

Alphabetical Alliterations

A variation of this is to begin each line with a different letter of the alphabet. It is probably too much to expect one child to write alliterations for the entire alphabet, so you can divide the class into groups and assign just some of the letters to each group. An example would be the following.

Amy aimed the arrow at an apple.

Boastful behavior bores even best buddies.

Cross crocodiles crouched candidly in the cattails.

Fred frequently furnished frightening folk tales and fantastic fables.

Numbered Alliterations

Another way to use alliteration in writing is to have students write ten different sentences, each one beginning with a different number. The letter or sound of the number at the beginning of the sentence is the letter or sound with which to begin the other words (or most of them). Here is an example:

One *wonderfully wild woodpecker wandered in the woods.*

Two *tired tourists trudged toward the twinkling tower.*

Six *sizable seagulls swooped skyward.*

Seven *self-conscious siblings sat on the scruffy sofa and sipped sodas silently.*

Ten *tenderhearted teenagers toasted a terrific teacher.*

Alliterative Creatures

Have students draw a picture of an extremely unusual animal or creature. They then describe their creatures by writing six lines. Each line is an alliterative sentence. The lines should include the following information.

title - The name of your creature

line 1 - Where your creature is from

line 2 - What your creature eats

line 3 - What your creature likes

line 4 - What your creature doesn't like

line 5 - What your creature did to or for you

Here is an example of an alliterative creature poem.

Silly Suzy

Silly Suzy survives in Satin Gully, South Dakota

Silly Suzy is satisfied with sweets and sunflower sandwiches

Silly Suzy likes sensational sapphires

Silly Suzy doesn't like sneaky snakes

Silly Suzy served me some shrimp scampi on Saturday

Using Spelling Words

Choose ten of your spelling words and have students write an alliterative sentence for each of them.

port - to carry

port: a place where ships may wait, load, or unload cargo

porter: one who carries things such as baggage

portable: can be carried

portfolio: a case for carrying loose papers and pictures

export: the act of carrying goods out of the country

import: to bring in goods, as from a foreign country

importer: one who brings in goods from a foreign country

deport: to send a person away; to banish

deportee: one who is sent away

report: an account of something that happened

reporter: one who brings news

support: to carry along with help

transport: act or means of carrying from place to place

vis or **vid** - to see

visible: can be seen

vision: something seen; the ability to see

envision: to see in one's mind

visor: a mask for the face; a brim on a hat to protect the eyes

visualize: to make visible; to bring into the mind something not present

invisible: cannot be seen

provide: to see what will be needed and supply it

Primary

- March is the third month of the year. It was the first month on the ancient Roman calendar. March has always had thirty-one days.
- The flowers for March are the violet and daffodil, and the birthstone is the aquamarine.

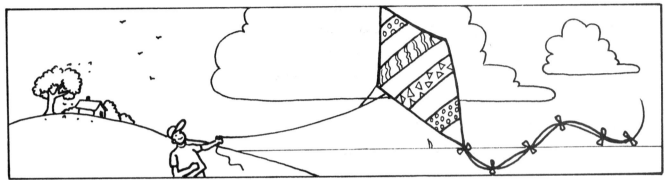

1. Ohio became the seventeenth U.S. state in 1803. Seven U.S. presidents were born in Ohio.

1. Nebraska became the thirty-seventh U.S. state in 1867. Nebraska has the only national forest completely planted by man.

1. Yellowstone National Park was established on this date in 1872. Yellowstone is the oldest United States national park.

1. The Peace Corps was established on this date in 1961 by President John F. Kennedy. Its purpose was to help developing nations.

1. Frédéric Chopin was a Polish pianist and composer. He was born on this day in 1810.

2. This is the birth date of Dr. Seuss, whose real name was Theodore Geisel. He was born in 1904. Seuss wrote The Cat in the Hat and many other books enjoyed by millions.

2. Sam Houston was an American political leader. He was born on this day in 1793. He fought for the independence of Texas from Mexico. The city of Houston was named after him.

2. In 1923 the first issue of a new magazine called Time was published.

3. On this day in 1847 Alexander Graham Bell was born. He is credited with inventing the telephone.

3. Florida became the twenty-seventh state on March 3, 1845. Florida has one of the largest swamps in the world.

3. The first laws to protect child workers were passed in the U.S. in 1842.

3. Author Patricia MacLachlan was born on this date. One of her famous books is Sarah, Plain and Tall.

3. On this date in 1931 Congress declared "The Star Spangled Banner" the national anthem of the U.S.

4. The U.S. Constitution went into effect on this date in 1789.

4. Vermont became the fourteenth U.S. state in 1791.

4. In 1917 Jeanette Rankin became the first woman to serve in Congress.

4. This date was Inauguration Day until 1937.

5. The Boston Massacre was an attack on American colonists by British troops. It occurred on this date in 1770.

6. Michelangelo was the most famous artist of the Italian Renaissance. He was born in 1475. He was a painter, sculptor, and architect.

6. Elizabeth Barrett Browning was an English poet. She was born on this day in 1806.

7. Luther Burbank was born on this day in 1849. Burbank was an American horticulturist who developed over two hundred plant varieties.

7. Alexander Graham Bell patented the telephone on this date in 1876. He sent the first message three days later. It was, "Come here, Watson. I want you."

9. This is the birth date of Amerigo Vespucci. He was an Italian navigator after whom America is named. He was born in 1451.

10. The Salvation Army was organized in the U.S. on this date in 1880.

12. Juliette Low founded the Girl Scout movement in America in 1912.

12. In 1664 King Charles II of England granted land in what is now New Jersey to his brother, the Duke of York.

13. Standard Time was established in the United States on this date.

13. The planet Uranus was discovered by German-English astronomer Sir William Herschel in 1781.

13. In 1852 the first cartoon symbolizing the U.S. as "Uncle Sam" appeared in the New York Lantern.

14. American Eli Whitney was granted a patent for the cotton gin in 1794.

14. March 14, 1879 is the birth date of Albert Einstein. He was the German-born scientist who won the Nobel Prize for physics.

15. For the first time in history a president, President Wilson, held an open press conference in 1913.

15. Andrew Jackson was the seventh president of the United States. He was born on this date in 1767. He was a firm believer in democracy.

15. On this day in 1820 Maine became the twenty-third state.

16. On this date in 1751 James Madison was born. He was our fourth president.

16. The first docking of one spacecraft with another was accomplished by the United States in 1966.

16. Georg S. Ohm was a German physicist who studied electric currents. He was born on this day in 1787.

16. Sid Fleischman is a famous children's author. He was born on this date.

17. This is St. Patrick Day. St. Patrick is the patron saint of Ireland. He died on March 17, 461 A.D.

17. Luther and Charlotte Gulick founded the Camp Fire Girls, an organization for young girls, in 1910.

18. The first person to walk in space was Soviet cosmonaut Aleksei Leonov. He did the space walk on this day in 1965.

18. Grover Cleveland was the twenty-second and twenty-fourth U.S. president. He was born on this day in 1837.

19. This is Swallow's Day. Every year for over a century, swallows have flown 2,000 miles to their nests in and near the mission of San Juan Capistrano, California.

20. This is the birth date of children's author Bill Martin. He was born in 1916. He wrote Brown Bear, Brown Bear, What Do You See.

21. This is the first day of spring in the Northern Hemisphere. It is the first day of fall in the Southern Hemisphere. Day and night are exactly twelve hours long all over the world.

21. German composer Johann Sebastian Bach was born on this date in 1685.

21. This is the birthday of Benito Juárez. He was born on this date in 1806. Juárez is considered the "George Washington" of Mexico.

22. Marcel Marceau is considered the world's best-known mime. He was born on this day in 1923.

23. In 1775 famous statesman Patrick Henry gave his "Give me liberty or give me death" speech.

23. In 1942 people of Japanese-American heritage living on the Pacific coast were moved to internment camps inland.

24. Today is the birthday of magician Harry Houdini.

26. The famous American poet Robert Frost was born on this day in 1874. Many children have read his poem, "Stopping by Woods on a Snowy Evening."

26. New Yorkers were amazed as they watched the first public demonstration of the making of pancakes in 1882.

26. This is the birth date of Sandra Day O'Connor. She was appointed to the Supreme Court in 1981. She is the first female ever to serve on this court.

27. Nathaniel Currier was an American lithographer. He was born on this date in 1813.

27. George Washington signed the act that created the United States Navy in 1794.

27. This is the birth date of German physicist Wilhelm Roentgen, who discovered the X ray. He was awarded the Nobel Prize in 1901.

27. On this day in 1964 Alaska experienced a major earthquake.

29. This is the birth date of John Tyler. He was the tenth U.S. president. He was born in 1790. During his term Texas was added to the territory acquired by the United States.

30. In 1858 Hyman Lipman received a patent for the first pencil with an eraser.

30. In 1867 Alaska was purchased from the Soviet Union. This was done much to the disappointment of many people who thought it was a foolish waste of money.

30. Vincent Van Gogh was a famous Dutch artist. He was born on this date in 1853.

30. Anna Sewell, author of Black Beauty, was born in England on this date in 1820.

30. The Fifteenth Amendment became part of the United States Constitution on this date in 1870. It forbids any state to deny citizens the right to vote because of race, color, or previous condition of servitude.

31. U.S. Daylight Savings Time began in 1918 and lasted two years. Following World War II, it was reestablished.

31. Franz Joseph Haydn was an Austrian composer of symphonies. He was born in 1732.

31. United States took possession of the Virgin Islands by purchasing them from Denmark in 1917.

31. In 1889 the famous landmark of Paris, France, the Eiffel Tower, officially opened in spite of many protests.

Upper Grades

- March is the third month of the year. It was the first month on the ancient Roman calendar. March has always had thirty-one days.
- The flower for March is the violet, and the birthstone is the aquamarine.
- March is Youth Art Month. Many famous artists were born in March.

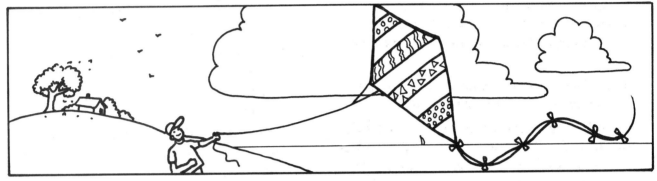

1. Ohio became the seventeenth U.S. state in 1803. Seven U.S. presidents were born in Ohio.

1. Nebraska became the thirty-seventh U.S. state in 1867. Nebraska has the only national forest completely planted by man.

1. Yellowstone National Park was established on this date in 1872. Yellowstone is the oldest United States national park.

1. The Peace Corps was established on this date in 1961 by President John F. Kennedy. The Peace Corps provides workers and teachers for developing nations. It also trains residents of these nations in modern methods.

1. Frédéric Chopin was born on this day in 1810. He was a Polish pianist and composer.

2. Sam Houston, American political leader, was born on this day in 1793. He fought for the independence of Texas from Mexico. Houston, Texas, was named after him.

2. This is the birth date of Dr. Seuss, whose real name was Theodore Geisel. He was born in 1904. Seuss wrote <u>The Cat in the Hat</u> and many other books enjoyed by millions.

2. On this day in 1923 the first issue of a new magazine called <u>Time</u> was published.

2. Texas declared its independence from Mexico on this day in 1836.

3. The Missouri Compromise was passed on this date in 1820.

3. On this day in 1847 Alexander Graham Bell was born. He invented the telephone.

3. Florida became the twenty-seventh state on March 3, 1845. Florida has more lakes than any other state and one of the largest swamps in the world.

3. In 1931 Congress declared "The Star Spangled Banner" as the national anthem of the U.S.

3. Patricia MacLachlan, author of books for young people, was born on this date. One of her famous books is <u>Sarah, Plain and Tall</u>.

3. The first laws to protect child workers were passed in the U.S. in 1842.

4. In 1917 the first woman to serve in Congress, Jeanette Rankin, took her seat in the House.

4. The United States Constitution went into effect on this date in 1789.

4. Vermont became the fourteenth U.S. state in 1791. Vermont's first constitution was written in 1777. It made Vermont a separate country. It said men could not own slaves and did not have to own property to vote.

4. William Penn received the land grant for what is now Pennsylvania in 1681.

5. The Boston Massacre took place on this date in 1770 when British soldiers fired on an angry Boston mob. A monument stands today with the words: "On that night the foundation of American Independence was laid."

5. James Ives, American painter and lithographer, was born on this date in 1824.

6. Michelangelo was born on this day in 1475. He is the most famous artist of the Italian Renaissance. He was a painter, sculptor, and architect.

6. English poet Elizabeth Barrett Browning was born on this day in 1806.

6. On this day in 1836 the siege of the Alamo ended after thirteen days, as the 200 Texans were finally overwhelmed by 3000 Mexican soldiers.

7. Luther Burbank was born on this day in 1849. Burbank was an American horticulturist who developed over two hundred plant varieties, including new types of potatoes, plums, berries, and flowers.

7. On this date in 1876 Alexander Graham Bell invented the telephone. Bell sent the first message three days later. The message was, "Come here, Watson. I want you."

9. Amerigo Vespucci, Italian navigator, was born on this day in 1451. America was named after him.

9. On this day in 1862 the Merrimack fought the Monitor.

10. The Salvation Army was organized in the United States on this date in 1880.

10. Harriet Tubman died on this day in 1913. She was born about 1821. She was an American abolitionist. She was called "Moses" because she led 300 black people to freedom between 1850 and 1860.

12. Juliette Low founded the American Girl Scout movement in 1912.

13. Standard Time was established in the United States on this day in 1884.

13. In 1852 the first cartoon symbolizing the U.S. government as "Uncle Sam" appeared in the New York Lantern.

13. The planet Uranus was discovered by German-English astronomer Sir William Herschel in 1781.

14. American Eli Whitney was granted a patent for the cotton gin in 1794. This machine could clean cotton faster than twenty-five workers.

14. March 14, 1879 is the birth date of Albert Einstein, the German-born scientist who won the Nobel Prize for physics. Einstein said, "Imagination is more important than knowledge."

14. Casey Jones, American railroad engineer, was born on this day in 1864. He gave his life to save the lives of his passengers and crew. A song was written about his skill and courage.

15. For the first time in history a president, President Wilson, held an open press conference in 1913.

15. Andrew Jackson, seventh president of the United States, was born on this date in 1767. He was a firm believer in democracy.

15. On this day in 1820 Maine became the twenty-third state.

15. The United States Military Academy was founded at West Point, New York on this date in 1802.

16. The first docking of one spacecraft with another was accomplished by the United States in 1966.

16. On this date in 1751 James Madison, the fourth president of the United States, was born. President Madison is often called the Father of the Constitution because he led the fight to add the first ten amendments, called the Bill of Rights.

16. Georg S. Ohm, German physicist who studied electric currents, was born on this day in 1787. The ohm, a unit of electric resistance, was named after him.

16. Dr. Robert Goddard, an American scientist, worked on figuring out how to send a ship into outer space. On March 16, 1926, he fired the first liquid-fuel rocket in history. It traveled less than 184 feet.

17. Ferdinand Magellan, captain of the first ships to sail around the world, discovered the Philippine Islands in 1521. He was killed there and didn't return home with his remaining ships.

17. On this day in 1776 the British evacuated Boston.

17. This is St. Patrick's Day. St. Patrick, the patron saint of Ireland, died on March 17, 461 A.D. Born in Britain, captured by pirates at age sixteen, and sold as a slave in Ireland for six years, he escaped, studied, and returned to Ireland to teach Christianity.

17. Luther and Charlotte Gulick founded the Camp Fire Girls in 1910.

18. The first person to walk in space was Soviet cosmonaut Alexei Leonov on this day in 1965.

18. Grover Cleveland, the twenty-second and twenty-fourth U.S. president, was born on this day in 1837. Cleveland worked hard for honest government.

19. This is Swallow's Day. Every year for over a century, swallows have flown 2,000 miles to their nests in and near the mission of San Juan Capistrano, California.

20. This is the birth date of children's author, Bill Martin. He was born in 1916. He wrote Brown Bear, Brown Bear, What Do You See. Mitsumasa Anno, Ellen Conford, Lois Lowry and Louis Sachar were also born on this day.

21. This is the first day of spring in the Northern Hemisphere. It is the first day of fall in the Southern Hemisphere. Day and night are exactly twelve hours long.

21. German composer Johann Sebastian Bach was born on this date in 1685.

21. This is the birthday of Benito Juárez. He was born on this date in 1806. Juárez is considered the "George Washington" of Mexico.

22. Marcel Marceau, the world's best-known mime, was born on this day in 1923.

22. Randolph Caldecott was born on this date in 1846. Caldecott was an English artist. The Caldecott Medal is named for him.

23. In 1775 famous statesman Patrick Henry gave his "Give me liberty or give me death" speech. He was born in 1874.

24. Today is the birthday of magician Harry Houdini.

26. The famous American poet Robert Frost was born on this day in 1874. Many children have read his poem, "Stopping by Woods on a Snowy Evening."

26. New Yorkers were amazed as they watched the first public demonstration of the making of pancakes in 1882.

26. This is the birth date of Sandra Day O'Connor. She was appointed to the Supreme Court in 1981. She is the first female ever to serve on this court.

27. Nathaniel Currier, American lithographer, was born on this date in 1813.

27. George Washington signed the act that created the United States Navy in 1794.

27. This is the birth date of German physicist Wilhelm Roentgen, who discovered the X ray. He was awarded the Nobel Prize in 1901.

27. On this day in 1964 Alaska experienced a major earthquake.

29. This is the birth date of John Tyler, tenth U.S. president, born in 1790. During his term Texas was added to the territory acquired by the United States.

30. In 1858 Hyman Lipman received a patent for the first pencil with an eraser.

30. In 1867 Alaska was purchased from the Soviet Union. This was done much to the disappointment of many people who thought it was a foolish waste of money.

30. Vincent Van Gogh, the famous Dutch artist, was born on this date in 1853.

30. Anna Sewell, author of Black Beauty, was born in England on this date in 1820.

30. The Fifteenth Amendment became part of the United States Constitution on this date in 1870. It forbids any state to deny citizens the right to vote because of race, color, or previous condition of servitude.

31. U.S. Daylight Savings Time began in 1918 and lasted two years. It was repealed due to the violent protests from farmers that their cows gave milk an hour after the milk trains had passed. Following World War II, it was reestablished.

31. Franz Joseph Haydn, Austrian composer of symphonies, was born in 1732.

31. United States took possession of the Virgin Islands by purchasing them from Denmark in 1917.

31. In 1889 the famous landmark of Paris, France, the Eiffel Tower, officially opened in spite of many protests.

Borrowing a Plot

Becoming Familiar with the Story

It is difficult for elementary-age students to come up with original plot ideas with interesting characters. There are times when you wish to have them drop themselves into a story that has already been written. A wonderful example is the Mary Calhoun book, *Hot Air Henry*, the story of a cat who accidentally lands in a hot-air balloon basket and has various adventures before returning to earth. Although this is a primary book, it can be used successfully with any level.

Writing Your Own Adventure

After reading the book to the students, have them discuss what adventures Henry had along the way, what the climax was, and what words were used by the author to describe hot-air balloons. Then have them imagine themselves in a situation where they have accidentally landed in a hot-air balloon basket. What adventures might they have, what would the climax be, and how would they get down? Remind them of all the fine descriptive writing they have done on previous assignments and how that descriptive writing would add to their story. Be sure to have them vividly describe getting into the basket. Some students are so anxious to tell about their flying adventures that they forget this part.

When the final drafts are completed on these stories, students may wish to design their own basket and balloon. They can draw an extremely large balloon on paper, draw a smaller one with their photo peering over the edge of the basket, or use a strawberry basket and paper-maché a balloon to make a three-dimensional model. Endless adventures are possible with this book.

Another Book to Use

Another successful book to use for this technique is Tomie de Paola's *Strega Nona*. Strega Nona's magic pasta pot goes wild when Big Anthony uses it without permission and doesn't know how to stop it from making pasta.

Have students consider how a different character might start something he can't stop without help. What would the adventures be along the way? How would this character finally stop the wild adventure? Read this book aloud to your students and let them use it as a stimulus for their own adventures.

Once you have used these books with your students, you will find many others that could be used the same way for this writing assignment.

A-Z All About Me

During the months of March and April have the students write about themselves using a different topic each day, starting with a topic that relates to the letter A and continuing through the alphabet. You may choose to have them write in their March journal or make a special journal with the topics printed on half-sheets of paper. Some teachers choose to have this as a rough draft copy and then have the students do a final version after the rough draft is edited by the teacher or parent helpers. This final version is put into a book that can be shared with parents at an open house. One of the most effective motivational tools is to share your example before the students start to write or to have a few students share theirs each day after everyone has completed the daily assignment. The topics for the two months are:

A What **animal** do you think is the most interesting animal in the world and why?

B What do you think some of the most **bothersome** things are?

C If you could **collect** anything, what would you choose and why?

D If you could sit in a soft chair and **daydream**, what would you daydream about?

E What are two things that you can't seem to get **enough** of?

F What are some of your **favorite** things to do with your family?

G Describe the **greatest** day you can think of. What would happen during this day?

H Who is your **hero** and why?

I Tell about a decision you made that was **important** or an **idea** you had that turned out to be **important**.

J What makes you more **jolly** than anything else?

K If you were **king**, what are some of the changes you would make?

L Think of a situation where you really **laughed** hard and write about it.

M If you have **moved**, what was it like; and if you haven't moved, write about what you think it would be like.

N Tell what the **number** one month of the year is for you and why.

O Tell about one of the jobs you might have when you are **older** and why you think this is a possibility.

P Describe a **person** you like and list some qualities that make you like this person.

Q If you could ask a famous person two **questions**, who would you choose and what would your questions be?

R If you could add some **rules** to your school, your home, your town, your country, or the world, what would these rules be?

S What is **sportsmanship**? Give examples of situations involving good sportsmanship.

T What are the **titles** of two of your favorite books and why are they favorites?

U Tell about something you think is **unforgettable**, something you will always remember.

V Invent a new **vitamin**. What is it called and how does it help you?

W What are three **wishes** you would like to have come true?

X What is a skill at which you would like to be **excellent**? (Yes, we're cheating here with the letter x.)

Y What will you remember most about this school **year**?

Z A **zephyr** is a soft, gentle breeze. If you were in a hot-air balloon being pushed by a zephyr, where would you like to go and what would you see there?

Poems to Memorize

2nd grade: "Spring Rain," by Marchette Chute, from *Random House Book of Poetry*, Random House. This poem is appropriate for this usually rainy month.

3rd grade: same as 2nd grade.

4th grade: "Since Hanna Moved Away," by Judith Viorst, from *Random House Book of Poetry,* Random House. If you ever had a friend move away, you'll understand Judith Viorst's feelings in this poem.

5th grade: "The Road Not Taken," by Robert Frost, from *American Poetry and Prose*, Houghton Mifflin. This poem points out that life is a series of choices that we all have to make.

6th grade: same as 5th grade.

Note your special poems for memorization

_____

_____

_____

_____

Poems to Write

This month features poems about people. Two different formats can be used. The subject of the poems can be friends, relatives, characters from books, people from history, or modern-day heroes.

Character Poem

This poem, using eight lines, describes a person. Each line provides specific information. The lines of the poem are:

line 1 - name

line 2 - three describing words

line 3 - relative or friend of

line 4 - who likes

line 5 - who wants

line 6 - who really

line 7 - resident of

line 8 - synonym

This is an example of a character poem to share with your class before they write their own poems.

Harriet Swan

Quiet, gentle, silly

Sister of Kenny and Melissa

Who likes pizza and chocolate ice cream

Who wants peace on earth

Who really wants to visit Disney World

Resident of Salt Lake City, Utah

Happy Harriet

Personal Poem

This is a wonderful idea for the first page in a book of poetry the student has written or an open house bulletin board display with the child's silhouette. You can also have students use it as a character description for a character from a book. The format for the poem is:

My name is _____

Another name I have is _____

The object in my heart is a _____ because

The word on my forehead is ____ because

A sound I love is the sound of_____

A smell I love is the smell of_____

My favorite time of day is_____ because

The animal inside me is a _____ because

I remember when . . . (complete using 1 to 3 sentences).

This is an example of a personal poem about a fictional character, Ramona Quimby.

Ramona

My name is Ramona Quimby.

Another name I have is Nosy.

The object in my heart is friend because I try to find one.

The word on my forehead is curious because I want to know everything.

A sound I love is the sound of my cat purring.

A smell I love is the smell of my new rubber boots.

My favorite time of day is when school starts because I plan on learning to read there.

The animal inside me is a monkey because I enjoy running and jumping.

I remember the day we had a substitute.

It was scary not to have my teacher.

quad - four

quadrangle: a flat figure with four angles and four sides

quadrant: one quarter of a circle

quadrille: a square dance for four couples

quadruped: an animal with four feet

quadruple: made up of four; four times as much

quadruplets: any of four children born at a single birth

poly - many

polyglot: speaking and understanding several languages

polygon: a flat, closed figure made up of straight lines, especially one having three or more sides

polysyllable: a word of four or more syllables

polytechnic: of or teaching many scientific and technical subjects

Polynesia: a scattered group of many islands in the central and south Pacific Ocean

in or **im** - not

inadequate: not enough; insufficient

inclement: not mild (usually used in regard to the weather)

intolerable: not able to be tolerated or endured

insatiable: cannot be satisfied; always wanting more

invisible: cannot be seen

imperfect: not perfect

immature: not grown, unripe

immoral: not of good character

immortal: not subject to death

Primary

- April is the fourth month of the year. It is named for *aprilis*, a Latin word meaning "to open." The special flowers for April are the sweet pea and the daisy. The birthstone for April is the diamond.

1. April Fools' Day is the first day of April. People often play harmless jokes on this day.

2. The first White House Easter Egg Roll took place on this day in 1877.

2. Hans Christian Andersen was born on this day in 1805. He was a Danish collector of fairy tales.

3. In 1869 the Pony Express began.

4. In 1818 the Congress ordered the U.S. flag to be redesigned.

5. Booker T. Washington was born on this day in 1856. He was a famous black American leader.

5. Josph Lister taught others to sterilize instruments for surgery in order to prevent infection. He was born on this day in 1827.

6. On April 6, 1909, Admiral Peary finally reached the North Pole after trying for years.

6. The first modern Olympic Games were held in Athens, Greece, in 1896.

9. The first public library was started in New Hampshire on April 9, 1833. This is National Library Week.

10. In 1790 the U.S. Patent Board was started to protect the rights of inventors.

12. Children's author Beverly Cleary was born in 1916. She wrote <u>Ramona the Pest</u>.

13. The first elephant brought to the United States came from Bengal, India, in 1796.

13. In 1743 our third president was born. His name was Thomas Jefferson.

14. Noah Webster completed <u>An American Dictionary of the English Language</u> after working twenty years. It had 70,000 entries.

15. Leonardo da Vinci was an Italian painter and scientist. He was born on this day in 1452.

18. In 1775 Paul Revere made his famous ride to alert people that 800 British soldiers were on their way.

18. In 1906 the famous earthquake in San Francisco shook the city. It destroyed half of it.

18. In 1953 baseball star Mickey Mantle hit a home run that traveled 565 feet. It was at that time the longest measured home run in big league history.

22. In 1823 the first pair of roller skates was patented.

24. In 1945 delegates from fifty nations met in San Francisco to create the United Nations.

25. In 1901 New York became the first state to require license plates on vehicles.

26. Today is the birthday of John James Audubon. He devoted his life to drawing and painting pictures of animals, especially birds.

26. Patricia Giff was born on this day in 1935. She is the author of <u>Fourth Grade Celebrity</u>.

29. In 1878 a Boston newspaper carried ads for a $3 telephone that was guaranteed to work for one mile.

29. The zipper was first patented in 1913.

30. In 1803 the U.S. purchased enough land from France to create thirteen new states.

Upper Grades

- April is the fourth month of the year. It is named for *aprilis*, a Latin word meaning "to open." The special flowers for April are the sweet pea and the daisy. The birthstone for April is the diamond.

1. April Fools' Day is the first day of April. In English-speaking countries people play absurd but harmless jokes on this day. The observance originated in France.

1. In 1931 Jackie Mitchell was the first woman in baseball history to be signed up as a regular member of an otherwise all-male team.

2. The first White House Easter Egg Roll took place on this day in 1877.

2. Hans Christian Andersen, Danish writer and collector of fairy tales, was born on this day in 1805. He died in 1875.

3. Washington Irving was born on this day in 1783. He was the American author of <u>Rip Van Winkle</u> and <u>The Legend of Sleepy Hollow</u>.

3. In 1860 the Pony Express began its short life of eighteen months. There were 157 stations from St. Joseph, Missouri, to Sacramento, California. It cost $2 to $10 per ounce to send a letter.

4. In 1818 the Congress ordered the U.S. flag to be redesigned.

5. Booker T. Washington was born on this day in 1856. He was born a slave in Hale's Ford, Virginia. He was an author and a leader in education.

5. Josph Lister was born on this day in 1827. Lister introduced sterilization of instruments before surgery. Before then, 50 percent of the patients died after surgery due to infection.

6. On April 6, 1909, Admiral Peary finally reached the North Pole after trying for years. Accompanying him were five other men. They stayed at the Pole for thirty hours, planted the American flag, and then left.

6. The first modern Olympic Games were held in Athens, Greece, in 1896. Thirteen countries participated. The first Olympic Games were held in 776 B.C.

6. The U.S. officially declared war against Germany in 1917. This marked the beginning of U.S. involvement in World War I.

7. Today is the birthday of William Wordsworth. He was an English poet who was born in 1770 and died in 1850.

8. In 1513 the Spanish explorer Ponce de León landed in Florida looking for the Fountain of Youth.

9. The first public library was founded in Peterboro, New Hampshire, on April 9, 1833. This is National Library Week.

9. General Robert E. Lee surrendered the Confederate Army to General Ulysses S. Grant in 1865.

10. In 1790 the U.S. Patent Board was established to protect the rights of inventors. On April 10, 1849, Walter Hunt invented the safety pin and obtained patent number 6281.

12. Children's author Gary Soto was born on this day in 1952 in Fresno, California.

12. Children's author Beverly Cleary was born on this day in 1916 in McMinnville, Oregon. Cleary is the author of <u>Ramona the Pest</u> and <u>The Mouse and the Motorcycle</u>.

12. The U.S. Civil War began at Fort Sumter in 1861 when Confederate forces fired in the harbor of Charleston, South Carolina.

12. Soviet Major Yuri A. Gagarin orbited Earth in 1961. He was the first human to travel in space when he was launched in the spaceship <u>Vostok</u> and made a single orbit of Earth in 89.1 minutes.

13. President Thomas Jefferson was the third president of the U.S. He was born on this day in 1743.

13. Marguerite Henry, author of <u>King of the Wind</u> and <u>Misty of Chincoteague,</u> was born on this day in 1902.

13. The first elephant to come to the United States was brought to New York City from Bengal, India, in 1796.

14. Abraham Lincoln was fatally wounded by J. W. Booth on this date in 1865. Lincoln died at 7:22 the following morning.

14. Noah Webster completed <u>An American Dictionary of the English Language</u> after working twenty years. It had 70,000 entries.

15. Leonardo da Vinci was an Italian painter, sculptor, and scientist who was born on this day in 1452. In order to protect his scientific discoveries, da Vinci described his inventions in code. He reversed each letter and wrote his sentences from right to left.

15. In 1912 the luxury liner <u>Titanic</u> struck an iceberg and sank on its maiden voyage from England to New York.

18. In 1775 Paul Revere made his famous ride to alert people that 800 British soldiers were on their way to Concord where the colonists had stored their gunpowder. In Massachusetts, Revere's ride is celebrated on the fourth Monday of April. The famous Boston Marathon is run then.

18. In 1906 an earthquake that resulted in many fires, destroyed half of San Francisco, killing almost 500 people, injuring 1500, and leaving a quarter million people homeless.

18. In 1953 baseball star Mickey Mantle hit a home run that traveled 565 feet. It was at that time the longest measured home run in big league history.

21. John Muir, American naturalist, was born on this day in 1838 in Scotland.

22. In 1823 the first pair of roller skates was patented.

23. President James Buchanan was born on this day in 1791. He was our fifteenth president.

23. William Shakespeare was born on this date in 1564. He was probably the greatest English poet and playwright of all time. He wrote <u>Hamlet</u>, <u>Macbeth</u>, <u>A Midsummer Night's Dream</u>, and many other famous plays.

24. During the War of 1812 the British burned the Capitol, the White House, and other buildings in Washington, D.C. This happened in 1814.

25. Guglielmo Marconi, inventor of wireless telegraphy, was born in 1874.

24. In 1945 delegates from fifty nations met in San Francisco to create the United Nations.

25. In 1901 New York became the first state to require license plates on vehicles.

26. Today is the birthday of John James Audubon. He devoted his life to drawing and painting pictures of animals, especially birds.

26. Patricia Giff was born on this day in 1935. She was a reading teacher and has written dozens of books. She is the author of Fourth Grade Celebrity.

27. Samuel Morse was born on this day in 1791. He was an American inventor.

27. President Ulysses S. Grant was born on this day in 1822. He was our eighteenth president.

28. Maryland became the seventh state in 1788.

28. President James Monroe was born on this day in 1758. He was the only president other than Washington to run unopposed.

29. In 1878 a Boston newspaper carried ads for a $3 telephone that was guaranteed to work for one mile. It also advertised a $5 telephone that was guaranteed to work for five miles.

29. The zipper was first patented in 1913.

29. The Chinese game Mah-Jongg was the craze in almost every state in 1923.

30. The U.S. purchased enough land from France on April 30, 1803, to create thirteen new states. It was purchased from Napoleon Bonaparte for four cents per acre. It was called the Louisiana Purchase.

Autobiographical Incident

This is an essay in which students describe an event in their lives that was memorable or made an impact on them. This is a powerful and motivating writing assignment. By breaking it down into the steps listed below, it becomes a manageable project.

1. **Brainstorm** - The first step in having the students write about an autobiographical incident is to brainstorm together major categories of events that have affected their families or them as individuals. These categories might include things like births of siblings, deaths in the family, moving, major illnesses or accidents (their own or ones that severely affected the family), divorces, changing schools, or finding a new best friend.

2. **Choose an Event** - After these major categories are listed on the board, choose one event that you would write about as if you were doing the assignment and explain how you would think, organize, write, revise, and edit your writing. Discuss how the details and descriptions make the incident more interesting to the reader and how the writer is to write it from a first person point of view.

3. **List Ideas** - Then have students jot down ideas about what they are going to write. At this point many students find that they really don't have enough information on a topic to make it a complete essay, and they then choose another topic.

4. **Begin Writing** - After they have written down a few ideas, you may either wish to have them begin writing, or they may need to organize in more detail.

5. **Read Around Groups** - When everyone is finished with a first draft a few days later, you may have them neatly rewrite their work for RAGs, Read Around Groups. In this activity, the students sit in groups of three or four (be sure you have a strong writer in each group). Everyone should have a clipboard and a pencil as well as the draft of his or her essay. Their job will be to read each draft and make gentle suggestions on each paper. Students should also remember to include positive comments. They may circle words they think are misspelled, put in a period or comma with a circle around it where they think it should be added, add capitals with circles around them where they think they are needed, and, of course, make comments in the margin.

Group Editing - Before the students do any of this, have the group edit a paper together with you on the overhead, making "remarks to grow on" and "remarks to glow on." When you feel that everyone understands this well, they will be ready to begin. Do remind students that people might make suggestions that don't work for them or are inaccurate. Remind them that everyone is trying hard to assist everyone else in the group and these corrections are done to help. Because the writer has the final say, he or she doesn't have to make all the suggested corrections on the final paper.

Correct - After the students have passed the papers to other group members and have received their own papers back, each writer is then to return to his or her desk and read over the correction suggestions and comments. Then, the writer is ready to begin a final draft.

There are many ways to do RAGs. In some classrooms each student reads orally while the others take notes and make "grow on" and "glow on" comments one by one before any papers are passed. Find the way that is comfortable for you and your students. It should be a positive experience.

6. **Final Drafts** - Students are now ready to complete their final drafts. The skills that they have covered this month have included organization, essay writing, point of view, editing, revising, and critiquing.

Poems to Memorize

2nd grade: "Smart," by Shel Silverstein, from *Where the Sidewalk Ends*, Harper & Row, is a funny poem all children enjoy about how a child trades his money for more coins but less value.

3rd grade: same as 2nd grade.

4th grade: "Give Me a Book," by Myra Cohn Livingston, from *Good Books, Good Times!* selected by Lee Bennett Hopkins, Harper & Row, is about the joy of burying yourself in a book.

5th grade: same as 4th grade.

6th grade: "Homework," by Jane Yolen, from *The Random House Book of Poetry*, Random House, is a poem sixth-graders identify with because it tackles something close to them.

Note your special poems for memorization

_____

_____

_____

_____

Poems to Write

Rhythm and Rhyme

This is another copy change type of poem. This lesson is based on the poem "Beans, Beans, Beans" by Lucia and James Hymes, *Hurray for Chocolate and Other Easy to Read Jingles*, Scholarship Books. Though the book is no longer in print, you may still be able to find a copy and read this poem to students, noting its repetitive, catchy rhythm.

The students will need to choose a category that has many items associated with it. Some topics that students have chosen in the past have been shoes, books, pies, horses, dogs, and breads. Begin by writing a poem as a group. Select a topic and brainstorm all the things that are associated with this topic. When you have collected all students' ideas, give them the following skeleton into which you can insert some of their words

line 1 - title (topic)

lines 2 - 5 - four lines of things associated with the topic, describing words or phrases

line 6 - "are some I like"

line 7 - "I do."

(second stanza)

line 8 - 11 - four lines of other things associated with the topic

line 12 - too.

(third stanza)

line 13 - 16 - four lines of other things associated with the topic

line 17 - "But my favorite one is"

line 18 - state a favorite.

Besides varying the subject matter and descriptive phrases, this poem could be changed by changing line 17 to "Best of all," "But the best one is," or "I like . . ." Below are examples of rhythm and rhyme poems.

Instruments

Happy violins,
double bell euphonium,
absolutely sweet sounding flute,
the very big tuba —
are some I like,
I do.

Black clarinet,
pretty piano,
the very strange saxophone,
strings on the guitar,
too.

Long trombone,
low bass —
don't forget the
singing harp.
Those are some,
but my favorite one
is
the trumpet.
by Kate Price

Pies

Big pies,
small pies,
nice juicy strawberry pies,
fat, plump peach pies
are some I like,
I do.

Chocolate pies,
apple pies
small crunchy pumpkin pies,
sweet, sour lemon pies,
too.

Blackberry pies,
huckleberry pies,
those are some,
but my favorite one
is
all of them!
by Michelle Blake

anti - against

antibiotic: a chemical substance produced by bacteria, fungi, etc., that can kill or stop the growth of germs

antibody: a protein that is formed in the body to react to foreign substances, such as toxins or bacteria

antidote: a substance that is taken to work against the effect of a poison

antifreeze: a liquid with a low freezing point, put in the water of automobile radiators to prevent freezing

antipathy: a great dislike; strong feeling against

antiseptic: preventing infection by killing germs

antithesis: the exact opposite

derm - skin

derma: the layer of skin just below the outer skin

dermatitis: a condition of the skin in which it becomes inflamed

epidermis: the outer layer of the skin of animals

dermatologist: a doctor who specializes in skin disorders and diseases

ultra - beyond, exceeding, extreme

ultra: going beyond the limits

ultracritical: overly critical

ultraism: an extreme point of view

ultralight: a very small, simple airplane

ultramarine: beyond the sea

ultramodern: very modern ideas or style

ultrasonic: supersonic; beyond sound

ultrastellar: beyond the stars

ultraviolet: outside the violet end of the visible light spectrum

ultra-ornate: too fancy

Primary

- May is the fifth month. It has always had thirty-one days. There are several stories about how this month was named. The most widely accepted one is that it was named for Maia, the Roman goddess of spring and growth.
- The hawthorn and the lily of the valley are the flowers of May. The birthstone is the emerald.

1. England, Wales, and Scotland joined to form Great Britain in 1707.

1. May Day is one of the oldest holidays.

1. May Day! May Day! is an international distress signal used by ships and aircraft.

1. In 1931 the Empire State Building was completed in New York City.

3. The first American medical school opened in Philadelphia in 1765.

3. In 1919 airplane passenger service was started from New York City to Atlantic City, New Jersey.

4. Horace Mann was the father of the public schools. He was born on this day in 1796.

5. In 1961 Commander Alan B. Shepard, Jr., was the first American space explorer.

5. Today is Cinco de Mayo, an important holiday in Mexico.

5. Nellie Bly went around the world in seventy-two days in 1889. She was a famous journalist.

6. The first postage stamp was issued in England on May 6, 1840.

7. Two famous composers were born on this day. They were Johannes Brahms and Peter Tchaikovsky.

8. Mother's Day is celebrated on the second Sunday in May.

8. Harry Truman was our thirty-third president. This is his birthday.

9. In 1926 the first flight over the North Pole took place.

10. In 1869 the last spike was driven in the transcontinental railroad. It connected the western and eastern parts of the country.

11. Minnesota became the thirty-second state on this date in 1858.

13. In 1607 Jamestown was established. It was the first permanent U.S. settlement.

14. Israel became an independent country on this day in 1948.

15. Frank Baum was the author of <u>The Wizard of Oz</u>. He was born on this day in 1856.

15. In 1930 United Airlines became the first airline to have flight attendants.

18. In 1647 Massachusetts was the first state to pass a law requiring children to attend school.

18. On this day in 1980 Mt. St. Helens in Washington erupted.

18. Lillian Hoban is a famous children's author. She was born on this day.

20. Charles Lindberg flew across the Atlantic Ocean in 1927. It took him thirty-three hours. He was the first person to do this.

21. Clara Barton founded the American Red Cross in 1881.

22. Children's author Arnold Lobel was born on this day in 1933.

23. South Carolina became the eighth state on this day in 1788.

23. Ben Franklin invented bifocal eyeglasses in 1785.

24. The Brooklyn Bridge was opened to traffic on this day in 1883.

26. This is the birthday of Dr. Sally Ride. She is a famous American astronaut. She was born in 1951.

29. President John F. Kennedy was born on this day in 1917.

29. Mt. Everest is the world's highest mountain. It was first climbed on this day in 1953.

30. Memorial Day is observed in honor of all war dead.

Upper Grades

- May is the fifth month. It has always had thirty-one days. There are several stories about how this month was named. The most widely accepted one is that it was named for Maia, the Roman goddess of spring and growth.

- The hawthorn and the lily of the valley are the flowers of May. The birthstone is the emerald.

1. England, Wales, and Scotland joined to form Great Britain in 1707.

1. May Day is one of the oldest holidays.

1. May Day! May Day! is an international distress signal used by ships and aircraft.

1. In 1931 the Empire State Building was completed in New York City. For years this 102-story building was famous for being the tallest structure in the world.

2. In 1970 Diane Crump became the first female jockey to ride the Kentucky Derby.

2. The first regular scheduling of commercial television programs was approved by the Federal Communications Commission in 1941.

3. The first American medical school opened in Philadelphia in 1765.

3. In 1919 airplane passenger service was started by Robert Hewett. Hewlett flew two passengers from New York City to Atlantic City, New Jersey.

4. In 1626 a Dutch colonizer, Peter Minuit, landed on Manhattan.

4. Horace Mann was the father of the public schools. He was born on this day in 1796.

4. On this day in 1776 invisible ink was first used in diplomatic correspondence. John Jay, a colonial leader, sent secret information to his brother in England by writing between the lines of his regular letter.

5. In 1961 Commander Alan B. Shepard, Jr., was the first American space explorer. He was rocketed 115 miles into space and landed 15 minutes later.

5. This is Cinco de Mayo. It is remembered as one of the important days in Mexico history. About 2000 Mexican soldiers fought and won a battle against 6000 French soldiers in 1862.

5. Nellie Bly, who went around the world in seventy-two days, started her trip on November 14, 1889. She was a famous journalist and crusader for women's rights.

6. "Penny Black," the first U. S. postage stamp, was issued on May 6, 1847.

7. Robert Browning, English poet and husband of Elizabeth Barrett Browning, was born on this day in 1812.

7. Composers Johannes Brahms was born in 1833.

111

7. Russian composer and conductor Peter Tchaikovsky was born on this day in 1840.

8. The Red Cross was founded in 1863 by Jean Henri Durant, whose birthday was today. This international organization provides medical care in times of war or natural disasters.

8. Harry Truman, the thirty-third president of the United States, became president when Roosevelt died. He was born on this day in 1884.

9. In 1914 Mother's Day became a public holiday. It is celebrated on the second Sunday in May.

9. In 1926 the first men flew over the North Pole. They were Commander Richard E. Byrd of the U.S. Navy and Floyd Bennett.

9. In 1933 Nazi leaders burned 25,000 books that were considered forbidden reading.

9. In 1502 Christopher Columbus began his fourth and last voyage.

10. In 1896 the last spike was driven into the transcontinental railroad, connecting the western and eastern parts of the country. This took place in Promontory, Utah. The golden spike united the Union Pacific and Central Pacific Railroads.

11. Minnesota became the thirty-second state on this date in 1858.

12. The famous English nurse Florence Nightingale was born on this day in 1820. She is regarded as the founder of modern nursing.

12. Edward Lear, English author of nonsense verse, was born in 1812.

13. In 1607 Jamestown was established. It was the first permanent U.S. settlement. It was built by English settlers.

14. Gabriel Fahrenheit, German physicist, was born on this day in 1686.

14. Edward Jenner, a British physician, performed the first vaccination against smallpox in 1796.

14. Lewis and Clark began their trip up the Missouri River from what is now St. Louis in 1804.

14. Israel became an independent country as the last British troops left Palestine in 1948.

15. In 1924 Congress passed a law restricting immigration to this country by creating quotas for various nationalities.

15. Frank Baum was the author of The Wizard of Oz. He was born on this day in 1856.

15. United Airlines introduced a new service for its passengers in 1930, flight attendants.

16. The first "Oscar" was awarded by the Academy of Motion Picture Arts and Sciences on this day in 1929.

17. The first Kentucky Derby horse race was held in 1875.

17. In 1954 the Supreme Court ruled that racial segregation in public schools was unconstitutional.

17. This is the birthday of children's author Gary Paulsen, who was born in Minneapolis, Minnesota, in 1939.

18. In 1674 Massachusetts was the first state to pass a law requiring children to attend school. At that time children between the ages of eight and fourteen were required to attend school for at least twelve weeks.

18. On this date Abraham Lincoln was nominated for the presidency for the first time.

18. On this day in 1980 Mt. St. Helens in Washington erupted.

18. Lillian Hoban, a famous children's author, was born on this day.

19. The first Ringling Brothers Circus appeared at Baraboo, Wisconsin, in 1884.

19. In 1928 fifty-one frogs entered the "Frog Jumping Jubilee" at Angels Camp in Calaveras County, California. The winner jumped 3 feet 4 inches. The origin of this contest is described in Mark Twain's story, <u>The Celebrated Jumping Frog of Calaveras County</u>.

20. At 7:40 A.M. on March 20, 1927, Charles Lindberg left New York in his plane, "The Spirit of St. Louis," to fly to Paris. A $25,000 prize was offered for the first solo nonstop flight. His plane had 451 gallons of gas, no lights, no heat, no radio, no automatic pilot, and no de-icing equipment. He arrived in Paris thirty-three hours later, where 100,000 people had gathered to greet him.

21. Clara Barton founded the American Red Cross in 1881.

21. The first bicycles were imported to the U.S. from England in 1819. These were called "swift-walkers." When pedals were invented, the name changed to "bone-crushers."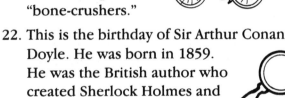

22. This is the birthday of Sir Arthur Conan Doyle. He was born in 1859. He was the British author who created Sherlock Holmes and Dr. Watson.

22. Mary Cassatt, famous American painter, was born on this day in 1844.

22. Children's author Arnold Lobel was born on this day in 1933.

23. South Carolina became the eighth state to ratify the Constitution on this day in 1788.

23. In 1785 Ben Franklin invented bifocal eyeglasses so he would not have to carry two pairs.

23. Scott O'Dell, author of <u>Island of the Blue Dolphins</u>, and Margaret Wise Brown, author of <u>Good Night Moon</u>, were born on this day.

24. The Brooklyn Bridge was opened to traffic on this day in 1883.

24. Queen Victoria of England was born on this day in 1819. Her birthday is celebrated as Commonwealth Day.

25. This is the birthday of Ralph Waldo Emerson, American poet. He was born in 1803.

26. President Andrew Johnson, who was on trial for impeachment charges, was acquitted by a single vote in 1868.

26. The first steamship to cross the Atlantic, the U.S.S. Savannah, did so in 1819. She made it largely with the help of her sails.

26. Astronaut Sally Ride was born on this day in 1951.

27. Julia Ward Howe, American poet who wrote "The Battle Hymn of the Republic," was born on this day in 1819. She was also a leader in the antislavery and women's vote movements.

27. Rachel Carson, American scientist and author, was born on this day in 1907. She was the author of <u>Silent Spring</u>, a book that provoked widespread controversy over pesticides.

28. Hernando de Soto landed in what is now Florida in 1539. He explored the Mississippi River later.

29. President John F. Kennedy was born on this day in 1917.

29. Mt. Everest, the world's highest mountain, was conquered in 1953 when two climbers, Edmond Hillary and Tensing Norkay, reached the top.

30. Memorial Day was first observed in 1868. Although it was originally set up as a legal holiday in many states to honor the memory of those who died in the Civil War, today it is observed in honor of all war dead.

31. Walt Whitman, American poet, was born on this day in 1819.

31. The Johnstown Flood happened in Pennsylvania in 1889. It killed thousands when a dam broke above the city.

Personal Interviews

This assignment involves not only writing, but also oral communication skills. Students must interview an older person and then write about that person's life when he or she was young. It's a good opportunity for students to see what life was like for a young person at a different point in time. This is an assignment that students will remember for a long time. By following the steps listed below, the project will be successful.

1. **Introduction** - First explain to your students that they are going to be interviewing someone who is older than they are – a grandparent, an older neighbor, or a family friend. They will be asking questions about what life was like when this person was a child and then writing an essay about this person's life.

2. **Develop Questions** - The second step is to develop the questions students will ask their interviewees. As a class, think of a list of questions and write them on the board. Some possible questions are "When you were a child my age . . ."

   - What was school like?
   - What were some of the school rules?
   - How was school different than it is now?
   - What clothes were fashionable when you were in school?
   - What music did you listen to?
   - What did you do in your spare time?
   - What chores did you have to do?
   - What fads were popular?
   - What are some ways life was better then?
   - What are some ways life is better now?

3. **Set Up Interview** - The students then need to contact the possible interviewee (with their parents' approval), explain about the interview, ask permission, and if it is granted:

   - set up a time
   - assemble a clipboard, two pencils, questions written on paper with large spaces between the questions for answers, and possibly a tape recorder
   - get approval on the questions to be asked.

4. **Begin Writing** - After the interview, the students are to organize the information into interesting written presentations. This should be modeled for them. Here is a possible beginning:

   Lucy Smith was nine years old in 1943. She remembers that a scary part of childhood was growing up during World War II. Because gasoline was rationed, cars weren't on the road often and most people walked around her small town. All the students walked to school even on rainy days.

   By modeling what we expect, we show the students that their essays are not to be in a question and answer format.

5. **Sharing** - You may want to have students read their papers orally to the class or in small groups when they are finished, thus giving them the opportunity to learn about life at other times and places as well as sharing their writing skills.

- *Tell about your favorite hobby. Tell how you got started, what skills or materials are required for your hobby, and where you're headed with it.*
- *This summer I plan to . . .*
- *A mistake I'll never make again*
- *The best memory of this school year will be*
- *Some of my favorite songs are . . . because . . .*
- *A famous person I wish I had known is . . .*
- *Pets are important because . . .*
- *Describe good sportsmanship and give an example of an incident when someone was a good sport.*
- *Some of the sounds I like hearing are . . .*
- *If I were one inch tall*

Poems to Memorize

For the month of May give the students two or three weeks to find a poem to present to the class. Remind them that the poem they choose must be at their grade level and that they must give you a written copy of it to read as they present it.

Poems to Write

The Important Thing Poems

This idea comes from the Margaret Wise Brown's book, *The Important Book*, Harper Trophy Books. In it she makes a statement about what is important about an item. Read the book to students and then ask them to select a topic and write a poem with the following form:

"The important thing about (topic)

is the _____."

Write several other lines that describe other elements of the topic.

End with "But the important thing about (topic)" (repeat line 1)

"is the _____" (repeat line 2)

On the following page is a sample of a student's work using the same form, but completely different ideas. When the students write their own poems, they are to choose three items, one for each stanza, and use the form indicated.

The Important Thing

The important thing about books
is the words.

There are princes and princesses
from all over the world,
and a kid who climbs a beanstalk.

With giants and people with
all different faces
and men and women
from all different places.

But the most important thing about books
is the words.

The important thing about music
is the sound —
the sound of the instruments
or the lyrics of the song,
or the voices of the singers,
or the beating of a drum,
and of course the playing
of a band.

But the important thing about music
is the sound.

The important thing about candy
is the taste —
the taste of a Milky Way
or a Hershey Bar
with cookies and cream
or a Butterfinger
or the nutty taste of a Payday
or even a Crunch Bar.

But the important thing about candy
is the taste.

by Kody Sacco, grade 4

ology - study or science of

biology: the science of plants and animals

geology: the study of the earth, including rocks and fossils

geography: the study of the face of the earth and how it is divided into continents, seas, and oceans

sociology: the study of society

paleontology: the study of life of the past geologic periods

anthropology: the study of humans and their origins

psychology: the study of the mind and behavior

meter - measuring device; one who measures

thermometer: a device for measuring temperature

audiometer: an instrument by which hearing can be measured

tachometer: a device to indicate speed of rotation

speedometer: a device to measure the speed of a vehicle

cred - believe

creed: a set of beliefs and principles

credible: can be believed

incredulous: not inclined to believe

accreditation: a certificate of acceptance

incredible: unbelievable

Primary and Upper Grades

- June is the sixth month of the year. Some authorities believe the Romans named the month for Juno, the patron goddess of marriage. Spring ends and summer begins around June 21 or 22 in the Northern Hemisphere. In the Southern Hemisphere, fall ends and winter begins during this month.

- The special flower for June is the rose. The gems for June are the pearl, alexandrite, and moonstone.

- The third Sunday in June is Father's Day.

1. Kentucky became the fifteenth state on this day in 1792.

1. Tennessee became the sixteenth state on this day in 1796.

2. The first baseball game played at night took place in Ft. Wayne, Indiana, in 1883.

2. P. T. Barnum's circus began its first tour of the United States in 1835.

3. In 1888 the poem "Casey at the Bat," written by Ernest L. Thayer, was published for the first time.

3. In 1965 two astronauts, James McDivitt and Edward White, began their four-day orbital flight in <u>Gemini Four</u>.

3. On this date in 1539 De Soto claimed Florida for Spain.

4. Henry Ford drove his first car around the streets of Detroit for the first time in 1896.

4. On this day in 1070 the first Roquefort cheese was accidentally invented by a monk in France. He returned to the lunch he had left uneaten several days before and found the sheep's milk cheese had developed a new flavor. He liked it so much he shared it with the other monks.

5. Today is the birthday of children's author Richard Scarry.

5. Bananas were introduced to visitors at the Centennial Exposition in Philadelphia. They were sold for ten cents each.

6. The first motion picture drive-in opened in Camden, New Jersey in 1933.

7. This is the birthday of Gwendolyn Brooks, the first black author to be awarded the Pulitzer Prize. She received it in 1950.

7. This is the birthday of Nikki Giovanni, poet.

8. The first vacuum cleaner was patented by Ives W. McGuffrey in 1869.

8. On this day in 1786 ice cream was first sold in New York City.

9. Donald Duck's "birthday" is today. He was created in 1934.

8. American architect Frank Lloyd Wright was born on this day in 1867.

10. In 1776 a committee made up of Thomas Jefferson, John Adams, Benjamin Franklin, Roger Sherman, and Robert R. Livingston was appointed to draft the Declaration of Independence.

10. Today is the birthday of Maurice Sendak, author of <u>Where the Wild Things Are</u>.

11. In 1859 the Comstock Silver Lode was discovered. This was one of the greatest silver discoveries of all time.

11. Jacques Cousteau, one of the greatest ocean explorers, was born on this day in 1910 in France.

11. Jeannette Rankin was born on this day in 1880. She was the first woman to serve in the United States House of Representatives.

12. Some people think that Abner Doubleday created the game of baseball in 1839, although most people think that it evolved from the games of cricket and rounders in the 1820s.

12. President George Bush was born on this day in 1924. He had been vice president for eight years before becoming president.

14. The Stars and Stripes officially became the United States flag in 1777. It had thirteen stars and thirteen stripes for the original thirteen colonies. Today we celebrate this day as Flag Day.

15. Charles Goodyear was granted a patent for rubber vulcanization in 1844.

15. Rembrandt, the famous Dutch painter, was born on this day in 1606.

15. On this day in 1836 Arkansas became the twenty-fifth state.

Miscellaneous Writing Ideas

June is a time when the school year is winding down, and your days are filled with end-of-the-year activities. You can still squeeze in several writing experiences, though. The following are fun writing assignments to round out the year.

※ ※

Thank-you letters

Have the students write thank-you letters to a friend, relative or an inventor. Have them thank this inventor and tell him or her what the invention means to them. Thank-you letters to friends or relatives should express gratitude for something this person has given or done for the writer. Thank-yous don't have to be just for presents. They can be for shared experiences or acts of kindness.

※ ※

Writing Directions

Have the students write step-by-step directions for getting from their house to school, cooking a favorite dish, or drawing a particular shape. Directions should be accurate and organized. It helps to list the directions or make a rough map before writing the detailed directions.

※ ※

Ingredient Story

Give students three elements and have them combine the elements into a story. Before writing, review the elements of a story (setting, characters, problem, climax, and ending) and remind students to use descriptive writing. Some elements you could use are:

- a detective, a missing ring, two kids
- an old diary, a hidden room, you and your best friend
- a disguised prince and a train
- an inventor, your school, a Saturday

※ ※

Similes

A simile is a figure of speech in which two unlike things are compared, usually using the words "like" and "as." Review some common similes like "happy as a clam," "hard as a rock," "grows like a weed," or "sings like a bird." Then have the students finish the following phrases to make original, clever comparisons.

- As soft as
- As rough as
- As pretty as
- As clever as
- As white as
- As dark as
- As quick as
- As warm as
- As smooth as
- As shiny as
- Jumps like
- Laughs like

Using Newspapers

You can use newspapers throughout the year. There are many ways they can be incorporated into your lessons to enhance writing skills as well as tie in skills and information in other areas of the curriculum. Below are some ideas you can use.

1. In three to four sentences, write a summary of an article.

2. Write a fairy tale as a news story.

3. Write three lost or found ads. Make each ad at least three lines long.

4. Find a job that appeals to you. Write a letter of application for that job, telling why you should be hired.

5. Write an editorial about why:

   • children should have safety lights on their bicycles

   • people should wear seat belts

   • runners should not wear headsets

   • some other issue you feel strongly about

6. Underline all the words in a sports article that pertain to the sport the article is about. Write a fictional sports article using these words.

7. Write an interesting ad to sell your bike.

Poems to Write

Cinquain

The cinquain is a five-line poem. It consists of the following lines:

    line 1 - title

    line 2 - two words describing the title

    line 3 - three words about action

    line 4 - four words conveying feeling

    line 5 - word related to title

After sharing the following examples, ask students to select their own topics and write cinquain poems. Some possible topics are ocean, lake, mountain, park, time of year, sport, holiday, or food.

Cat

Cat

sleek, quiet

stalking, purring, sleeping

always content and alert

Tracy

Summer

Summer

hot, fun

eating, playing, swimming

enjoying time with family

July

graphy - written about

biography: the written account of another person's life

autobiography: an account of a person's life written by himself or herself

autograph: a person's signature

calligraphy: the art of elegant handwriting

graph: something written; a diagram

scope - to watch or see

fluoroscope: an instrument used to observe the interior of things

microscope: an instrument to view things too small to be seen with the naked eye

periscope: an instrument for viewing all sides

stethoscope: an instrument for hearing faint sounds like heartbeats

telescope: an instrument for viewing distant objects

feder, fide, or **fid** - trust or faith

bona fide: in good faith; genuine

confide: to have trust in someone

confident: trust in oneself; self-reliant

confidential: entrusted with private or secret matters

federal: united under a common trust

fidelity: faithfulness

infidel: one who has no faith

Answers

Experts of the Dictionary - Novice

page numbers will vary

1. sulky - travel
2. gondola - travel
3. surrey - travel
4. hansom - travel
5. doublet - wear
6. howdah - travel
7. ascot - wear
8. kilt - wear
9. epaulet - wear
10. obi - wear
11. fez - wear
12. kayak - travel
13. toboggan - travel
14. umiak -travel
15. jerkin - wear
16 - jodhpurs - wear
17. victoria - travel
18. derby - wear

Experts of the Dictionary - Apprentice

pages will vary.

Parts of the Body

orb

sternum

palate

pharynx

ulna

epiglottis

Music Terms

frets

lute

oboe

sitar

fife

viola

zither

dulcimer

piccolo

Boat Terms

yawl

gaff

scull

prow

tacking

Experts of the Dictionary - Expert

Animals

sloth

lemur

peccary

kudu

ibex

Tools

hod

plumb

winch

trowel

scythe

awl

gimlet

Birds

petrel

emu

wren

tanager

shrike

osprey

grouse

skua